MASSAGE
BASICS

A Guide

to Swedish,

Shiatsu, and

Reflexology

Techniques

Mark F. **Beck**

Shelley **Hess**

Erica **Miller**

DELMAR

THOMSON LEARNING

Australia   Canada   Mexico   Singapore   Spain   United Kingdom   United States

PERSONAL CARE COLLECTION

Delmar Staff:

Business Unit Director: Susan L. Simpfenderfer
Executive Editor: Marlene McHugh Pratt
Acquisitions Editor: Paul Drougas
Developmental Editor: Patricia A. Gillivan

Editorial Assistant: Rebecca McCarthy
Executive Marketing Manager: Donna J. Lewis
Channel Manager: Wendy E. Mapstone
Executive Production Manager: Wendy A. Troeger

Library of Congress Cataloging-in-Publication Data
Beck, Mark
    Massage basics : a guide to Swedish, shiatsu, and reflexology techniques / Mark F. Beck, Shelley Hess, Erica Miller.
      p. cm.
    Includes index.
    ISBN 0-7668-3760-2
    1. Massage. I. Hess, Shelley, 1954-   . II. Miller, Erica T. III. Title.
  RA780.5 .B43 2001
  615.8'22—dc21   2001037236

Contents

Massage

Massage is said to be the most natural and instinctive means of relieving pain and discomfort. When a person has sore, aching muscles; abdominal pains; a bruise; or a wound, it is a natural and instinctive impulse to touch, press, and rub that part of the body to obtain relief.

With the decline of the use of massage in traditional medicine, a surge of interest in the use and value of massage has developed among paraprofessionals and the lay public. Several factors precipitated this trend. Increased awareness of physical and mental fitness, as well as the increasing cost of traditional medicine, opened the way for viable alternatives in healthcare. The development of the wellness model, which placed more emphasis on prevention and recognized the importance of controlling stress, advocated the value of massage. The psychological benefits of touch and its proven use in the treatment of pain returned massage to a place of prominence in the healthcare system.

MASSAGE SYSTEMS

The methods of massage generally in use today descend directly from the Swedish, German, French, English, Chinese, and Japanese systems.

1. The Swedish system is based on the Western concepts of anatomy and physiology and employs the traditional manipulative techniques of effleurage, petrissage, vibration, friction, and tapotement. The Swedish system also employs movements that can be slow and gentle, vigorous, or bracing, depending on the results the practitioner wishes to achieve.

2. The German method incorporates many of the Swedish movements and emphasizes the use of various kinds of therapeutic baths.

3. The French and English systems also employ many of the Swedish movements for body massage. Many excellent facial massage and beauty therapy treatments originated in France and England.

4. Acupressure stems from the Chinese medical practice of acupuncture. It is based on the Traditional Oriental Medical principles for assessing and treating the physical and energetic body and employs various methods of stimulating acupuncture points in order to regulate *chi* (the life force energy). The aim of this method is to achieve therapeutic changes in the person being treated as well as relieve pain, discomfort, or other physiological imbalances.

5. The Japanese system, called *shiatsu,* is a finger pressure method based on the Oriental concept that the body has a series of energy (*tsubo*) points. When pressure is properly applied to these points, circulation is improved and nerves are stimulated. This system is said to improve body metabolism and to relieve a number of physical disorders.

The following are additional systems that have gained recognition as beneficial forms of massage.

Sports massage refers to a method of massage designed especially to prepare an athlete for an upcoming event and to aid in the body's regenerative and restorative capacities following a rigorous workout or competition. This is achieved through specialized manipulations that stimulate circulation of the blood and lymph. Some sports massage movements are designed to break down lesions and adhesions or reduce fatigue. Sports massage generally follows the Swedish system, with variations of movements applied according to the judgment of the practitioner and the results he or she wants to achieve. Sports teams, especially those in professional baseball, football, basketball, hockey, ice skating, and swimming, often retain a professionally trained massage practitioner. Athletes, dancers, and others who must keep muscles strong and supple are often instructed in automassage, or massaging one's own muscles, and in basic massage on a partner.

Polarity therapy is a method developed by Randolph Stone (1890–1971) using massage manipulations derived from both Eastern and Western practices. Exercises and thinking practices are included to balance the body both physically and energetically.

The Trager method was developed by Dr. Milton Trager. This method uses movement exercises called mentastics along with massage-like, gentle shaking of different parts of the body to eliminate and prevent pent-up tensions.

Rolfing® is a systematic program developed out of the technique of structural integration by Dr. Ida Rolf. Rolfing aligns the major body segments through manipulation of the fascia or the connective tissue.

The method of reflexology originated with the Chinese and is based on the idea that stimulation of particular points on the surface of the body has an effect on other areas or organs of the body. Dr. William Fitzgerald is credited with first demonstrating the effects of reflexology in the early 1900s. Eunice Ingham worked for Dr. Fitzgerald and later, in the 1930s, she systemized the technique (popular today) that focuses mainly on the hands and feet.

Touch for Health is a simplified form of applied kinesiology, or principles of anatomy in relation to human movement. Developed by Dr. John Thie, D.C., this method involves techniques from both Eastern and Western origins. Its purpose is to relieve stress on muscles and internal organs. There are also a number of styles of bodywork and alternative health-related practices that use specialized kinesiology (a form of muscle testing) to derive information about the conditions of the body or how a particular substance or type of treatment might affect it.

Although there are many excellent massage methods, the Swedish system is still the most widely practiced, and is incorporated into many other procedures. Whatever method is used, it is essential to have a thorough knowledge of all technical movements and their effects on the various body systems.

Massage Movements

It is important to understand the movement to be applied to a particular part of the body. For example

- Light movements are applied over thin tissues or over bony parts.
- Heavy movements are indicated for thick tissues or fleshy parts.
- Gentle movements are applied with a slow rhythm and are soothing and relaxing.
- Vigorous movements are applied in a quick rhythm and are stimulating.

While applying the movements, pay close attention to the overall response of the recipient as well as the response of the tissue or body part to which the manipulation is being applied, and adjust the application accordingly.

An important rule in Swedish massage is that most manipulations are directed toward the heart (centripetal). Many massage techniques are intended to enhance venous blood and lymph flow and therefore are directed toward the heart and other eliminative organs. Only strokes light enough to not affect fluid flow may be directed away from the heart. When a massage movement is directed away from the heart, it is said to be centrifugal.

APPLICATION OF MASSAGE STROKES

Touch

Touch may be in the form of a handshake or a pat on the shoulder and is the primary communication tool used during massage. All massage techniques use physical contact, but the quality and sense of touch convey the intent and the power of the movements.

Light or superficial touch is purposeful contact in which the natural and evenly distributed weight of your finger, fingers, or hand is applied on a given area of the recipient's body. The size of that area may be regulated as necessary by using one or more fingers, the entire hand, or both hands. Touch can be remarkably effective in reducing pain, lowering blood pressure, controlling nervous irritability, or reassuring a nervous, tense person. The main objective of light touch is to soothe and to provide a comforting connection that is calming and allows the powerful healing mechanisms of the body to function.

DEEP TOUCH USING PRESSURE

Deep touch is performed with one finger, the thumb, several fingers, or the entire hand. The heel of the hand, knuckles, or elbow can be used according to desired results. The application of deep pressure is used when calming, anesthetizing, or stimulating effects are desired. Deep pressure may be used with other techniques such as cross-fiber friction, compression, or vibration. Deep pressure is useful in soothing muscle spasms and relieving pain at reflex areas, stress points in tendons, and trigger points in muscles. In addition to extensive use in trigger-point therapy, deep pressure is a technique often applied in reflexology, sport massage, acupressure, and *shiatzu*. When using deep pressure, caution must be used to stay within the pain tolerance of the recipient. In addition, good body mechanics must be used when applying deep pressure to prevent injury. Do not strain or hyperextend any joint. Deliver the pressure through body movement rather than simply hand and upper-body strength. See Figure 2-1a through e.

Gliding Movements

Gliding may be done using a varying amount of pressure and length of stroke. Gliding strokes glide over the recipient's entire body, body part (arm or leg), or specific area (muscle or reflex).

ETHEREAL BODY OR AURA STROKING

This type of stroking is done with long, smooth strokes in which your hands glide the length of the recipient's entire body or body part, coming very close to but not actually touching the body surface. Generally the movement is in one direction only, with the return stroke being farther

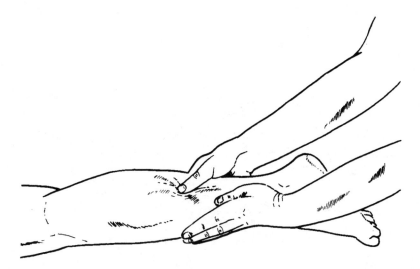

FIGURE 2-1a Deep touch using thumb. Notice the alignment of the thumb and arm to ensure that pressure is directed into the recipient with minimal stress to your joints.

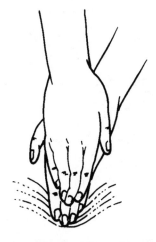

FIGURE 2-1b Deep pressure applied with braced fingers.

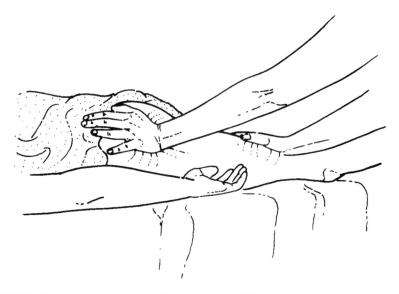

FIGURE 2-1c Deep touch applied with the heel of the hand.

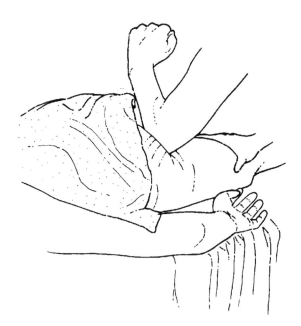

FIGURE 2-1d Deep touch applied with the elbow.

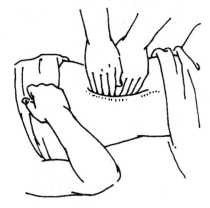

FIGURE 2-1e Deep pressure to the abdominal area.

from the body. The intention is to affect the energy fields that, according to some philosophies, surround or permeate the body. The direction of the stroking may be along the surface of the body to enhance or impede the natural flow.

The application of this soothing stroke is done only when the surrounding circumstances are very quiet and relaxed, and the recipient is receptive. It is sometimes used as the final stroke of a massage. See Figure 2-2.

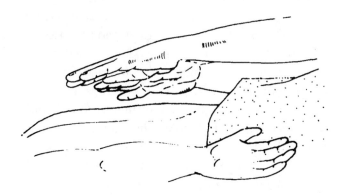

FIGURE 2-2 Ethereal or aura strokes do not touch the surface of the recipient's body.

FIGURE 2-3 Feather strokes (nerve strokes) use the lightest touch of the fingertips.

FEATHER STROKING

Feather-stroking movements use very light pressure of the fingertips or hands with long flowing strokes. Sometimes called "nerve stroking," it is usually done from the center outward and is used as a final stroke to individual areas of the body. Two or three such strokes will have a slightly stimulating effect on the nerves, while many repetitions will have a more sedating response. See Figure 2-3.

GLIDING OR EFFLEURAGE

Effleurage is a succession of strokes applied by gliding the hand over a somewhat extended portion of the body. There are two varieties of effleurage: superficial and deep. Superficial gliding strokes employ a very light touch. In gliding strokes, the pressure becomes firmer as the hand glides over the surface of the body. The technique of effleurage or gliding is accomplished with the fingers, the thumbs, the palm of the hand, the knuckles, or the forearm. Over large surfaces, such as the limbs, back, chest, and abdomen, the gliding movement is performed with the palm of one or both hands. Over small areas, such as the eyes or hands, the movement is performed with the fingers or thumbs. For very deep gliding strokes, the palms of the hands, the fingertips, the thumbs, the knuckles, or sometimes the forearms are used.

Superficial gliding strokes are generally applied prior to any other movement. Your hand is flexible yet firm and controlled so that as it glides over the body, it conforms to the body contours in such a way that there is equal pressure applied to the body from every part of the hand. Light strokes are used to distribute any lubricant that may be used and to prepare the area for other techniques. As your hands glide over the tissues, they sense variations that indicate where specific techniques will be applied. Effleurage is interspersed with other techniques to clear the area and soothe the intensity of some deeper manipulations. Slow, gentle, and rhythmic movements produce soothing effects. Rhythmic strokes should be applied in the direction of the venous and lymphatic flow.

Although superficial stroking appears to be simple, its technique is mastered only by long practice. Your hand should be relaxed in order to mold the surface of the body part being massaged. The pressure and speed of movement should remain constant. Upon completion of the stroke, your hand may be elevated and directed to the starting point. In some cases, the hands stay in contact by exerting more pressure centripetally (toward the heart) and then reducing the pressure and lightly stroking (feather stroking) the body to return to the starting point of the stroke. In this way you always maintain contact with the recipient.

Superficial gliding strokes are a valuable application for overcoming a general tired feeling or restlessness. This movement is particularly soothing to nervous or irritated people. Nervous headaches and insomnia (sleeplessness) are often relieved by gentle gliding strokes on the forehead.

DEEP GLIDING

Deep gliding uses enough pressure to have a mechanical effect. The depth of the gliding movement depends on three factors: the pressure exerted, the part of the hand or arm used, and the intention with which the manipulation is applied. Deep gliding strokes do not involve the use of excessive force. The pressure should never be so forceful as to cause bruising or injury to the tissues. Deep gliding strokes are especially valuable when applied to the muscles. It is most effective when the part under treatment is in a state of relaxation. Then the slightest pressure of the surface will be transmitted to the deeper structures. Deep gliding strokes have a stretching and broadening effect on muscle tissue and fascia. They also enhance the venous blood and lymph flow. If too much force is used, the recipient's body will respond with a protective reflex that will cause muscles to contract, thereby negating the desired effects. Deep gliding strokes generally follow the direction of the muscle fibers. On the extremities, the movements are always directed from the end of a limb toward the center of the body. Generally the movement is toward the heart or in the direction of venous and lymph flow, with the return stroke being much lighter and away from the center of the body. The exception to this rule is deep, short strokes applied to the muscle attachments and tendons. When directed from the tendon towards the muscle belly, these strokes tend to stretch the tendon and cause a reflexive relaxation of the muscle. Indications for the use of deep gliding strokes may include increasing fluid movement, stretching underlying tissues, separating and broadening tissues, increasing relaxation, and palpating deeper tissues. See Figure 2-4a through g and Figure 2-5a through g.

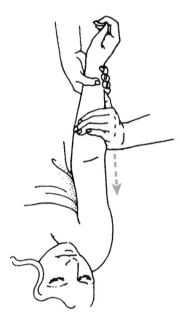

FIGURE 2-4a Effleurage or gliding strokes are applied in the direction of venous blood and lymph flow.

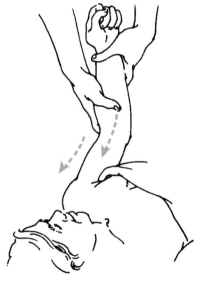

FIGURE 2-4b A V-stroke can be used for superficial or deep gliding strokes.

FIGURE 2-4c Apply digital effleurage to the forehead.

FIGURE 2-4d Direction of effleurage on the lower leg. The same upward movements are applied when massaging the back of the lower leg.

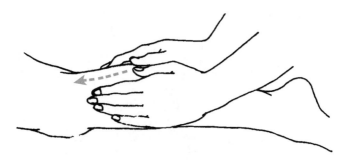

FIGURE 2-4e Stroke the leg with two hands.

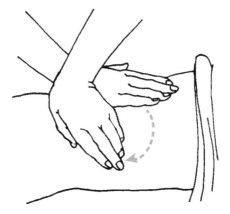

FIGURE 2-4f Stroke the abdomen in a deep circular movement.

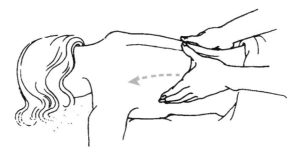

FIGURE 2-4g Stroke the entire back.

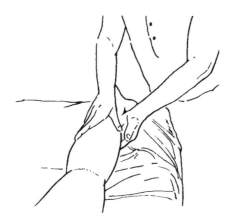

FIGURE 2-5a V-stroke applied to the posterior leg.

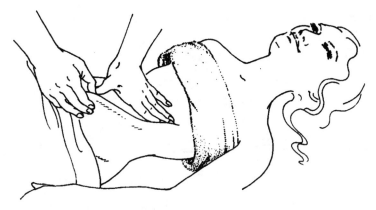

FIGURE 2-5b Apply deep circular effleurage following the path of the colon.

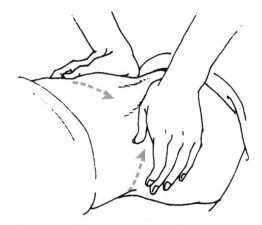

FIGURE 2-5c Inward deep gliding strokes of muscles over the stomach area and the abdominal region.

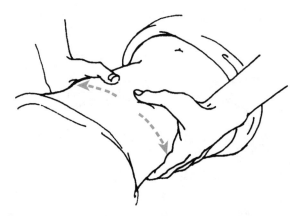

FIGURE 2-5d Outward deep gliding strokes to the muscles of the stomach area and the abdominal region.

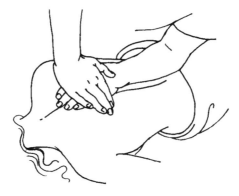

FIGURE 2-5e Apply two-handed (deep) effleurage around the scapula. Note that one hand is on top of the other.

FIGURE 2-5f Apply deep stroking under the scapula followed by rotation of the shoulder.

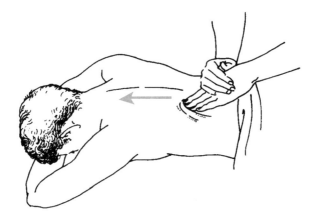

FIGURE 2-5g Deep gliding strokes with braced fingers.

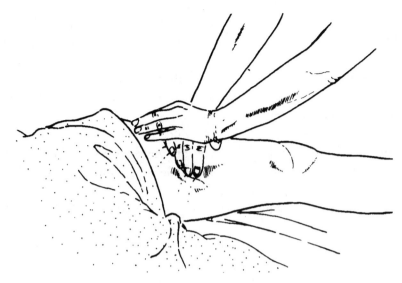

FIGURE 2-6 When using deep techniques, use good body mechanics to direct the manipulation into the recipient and at the same time protect yourself from injury.

When using deep gliding strokes, use good body mechanics to prevent strain and overuse syndrome injuries. Hand and arm positions should direct the force of the manipulation into the recipient. Keep your shoulders down and relaxed, and avoid hyperextending the wrists, fingers, or thumbs. See Figure 2-6.

Kneading Movements or Petrissage

In Swedish massage, kneading or petrissage is used on all fleshy areas of the body. Like deep gliding, kneading enhances the fluid movement in the deeper tissues. Skillfully applied, kneading helps reduce adhesions and stretch muscle tissue and fascia. In this movement, the skin and muscular tissues are raised from their ordinary position and then squeezed, rolled, or pinched with a firm pressure, usually in a circular direction.

On large areas of the body, both hands work alternately as a unit. The tissue is lifted with the palm of the fingers of one hand into the palm of the other hand. Then the process is reversed so the fingers of the other hand lift the tissue into the palm and base of the opposite hand. The hands alternate in a rhythmical, circular pattern over the entire body part being massaged. Over smaller structures, such as the arms, the flesh is grasped between the fingers and heel of the hand or the thumb. In both cases the maximum amount of flesh is drawn up into the palm and gently and firmly pressed and squeezed as if milking the deep fluids. On an area such as the arm, one hand may be used to apply the manipulation while the other hand stabilizes the arm, or both hands may alternate grasping the tissue on each side of the arm. Over smaller structures, such as the hands or fingers, the flesh is held between the thumb and fingers.

Fulling is a kneading technique in which you attempt to grasp the tissue and gently lift and spread it out, as if to make more space between the layers of tissue or muscle fibers. Often done with both hands simultaneously, the fleshy body part is gathered up between two hands, then raised and separated by the palms and thumbs as it is gently stretched across the fibers of the tissue.

Skin rolling is a variation of kneading in which only the skin and subcutaneous tissue is picked up between the thumbs and fingers and rolled. As the fingers alternately and continuously pick up and pull the skin away from the deeper tissues, the thumb glides along in the direction of the movement stretching the underlying fascia. Skin rolling warms, stretches, and begins to separate adhesions between fascial sheaths. When beginning to learn this technique, it is best to use both hands. Use NO lubricant for the technique. Gather up a roll of skin between the thumb and fingers. Continue to gather in more skin with the fingers as you slowly progress along the surface of the body. The thumb supports the roll of skin and slowly slides along as more skin is picked up by the fingers. See Figures 2-7a through e, 2-8, and 2-9.

Friction

Friction movements involve moving more superficial layers of flesh against the deeper tissues. Whereas kneading is done by lifting and pulling the flesh away from the skeletal structures and squeezing in such a way as to milk out the body fluids, friction presses one layer of tissue against another layer in order to flatten, broaden, or stretch the tissue. Friction is done in such a way that it also increases heat. As heat increases, the metabolic rate increases. Friction also increases the rate at which exchanges take place between the cells and the interstitial fluids (fluids situated between the cells and vessels in the tissues of an organ or body part). The added heat and energy also affect the connective tissue surrounding the muscles, making them more pliable so they function more efficiently.

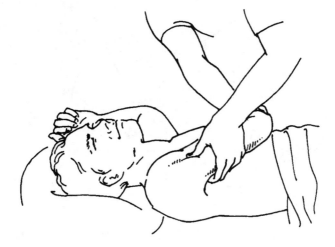

FIGURE 2-7a Kneading the triceps.

FIGURE 2-7b Kneading the calf muscles.

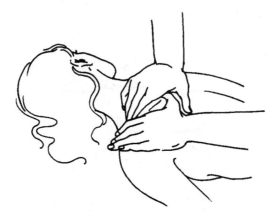

FIGURE 2-7c Petrissage includes the trapezius muscles.

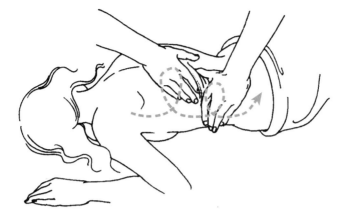

FIGURE 2-7d Apply petrissage to the entire side that is opposite you. This takes several passes.

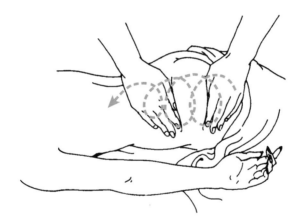

FIGURE 2-7e Apply kneading over the gluteals.

FIGURE 2-8 For fulling movement, grasp the flesh between the fingers and palms of the hand.

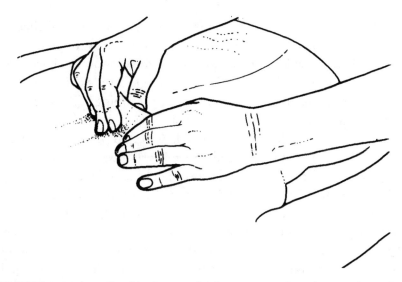

FIGURE 2-9 Skin rolling lifts the superficial tissues away from the muscles and other deeper tissues.

Friction helps to separate the tissues and to break down adhesions and fibrosis, especially in muscle tissue and fascia. It softens the amorphous (massed) ground substance between layers of fascia. Friction also aids in absorption of the fluid around the joints. Friction has a marked influence on the circulation and glandular activity of the skin. With friction strokes the area usually becomes red. This indicates an increased flow of blood to the area and more blood being rushed to the surface of the skin.

Friction strokes involve moving a more superficial layer of tissue against deeper layers of tissue. This requires pressure on the skin while it is being moved over its underlying structures. The skin and the hand move as a unit against the deeper tissues. Over muscular parts or fleshy layers, friction is applied with the palms of the hands, the flat of the fingers, or the thumbs. Over small surfaces, friction is applied with the fleshly parts of the fingertips or thumbs.

Friction movements may be circular or directional. In circular friction the fingers or the palm of the hand contact the skin to move it in a circular pattern over the deeper tissues. Circular friction is intended to produce heat and stretch and soften the fascia. Circular friction is a general stroke used to warm the area in preparation for more specific or deeper work. The palm or pads of the fingers make contact with the skin and move the skin and more superficial tissues over the deeper layers in a small circular pattern. The fingers or hand DO NOT slide over the skin in a circular manner, although the hand may move along to cover an extended area with circular friction. The intent is to move one layer of tissue over a deeper layer, resulting in a gentle stretching and warming of the area.

Circular friction is also valuable for palpating an area when assessing the condition of the underlying tissues. When working deeply on an area, circular friction and superficial gliding strokes are useful to soothe and calm the recipient before, after, and between deep techniques.

Directional friction may be either cross-fiber or longitudinal friction. Cross-fiber friction, as the name implies, is applied in a transverse direction across the muscle, tendon, or ligament fibers. Cross-fiber friction is usually applied with the tips of the fingers or the thumb directly to the specific site of a lesion. The intention of cross-fiber friction is to broaden, separate, and align the fibrous tissue. The stroke is broad enough to cover the tissue and deep enough to reach the tissue. When massaging a fibrous band, the cross-fiber friction stroke is not so broad that it snaps across the fiber. The fingers do not move over the skin but move the skin and superficial tissues across the target tissue.

In longitudinal friction, the hand moves in the same direction as the tissue fibers. This tends to stretch the tissue and align the collagen fibrils within the fascia.

Another form of friction sometimes classified by itself is compression. As the name implies, compression is rhythmic pressing movements directed into muscle tissue by either the hand or fingers. Palmar compression is done with the whole hand (palm side) or the heel of the hand over the large area of the body. Palmar compression is a rhythmical pumping action directed into the muscle perpendicular to the body part. Compression movements cause increased circulation and a lasting hyperemia in the tissue. Compression is a popular movement used in pre-event sports massage. The intention is to bring more blood and fluid into the tissues, preparing them to exert maximum energy sooner and for a longer period of time. See Figure 2-10.

Other manipulations that are considered friction include rolling, wringing, chucking, shaking, and vibration. Chucking, rolling, wringing, and shaking are variations of friction employed principally to massage the arms and legs.

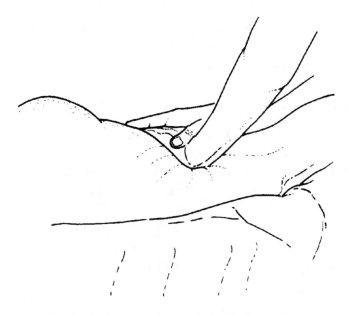

FIGURE 2-10 Two-handed compression applied to the hamstrings.

ROLLING

Rolling is a rapid back-and-forth movement with the hands, in which the flesh is shaken and rolled around the axis, or the imaginary centerline of the body part. The intention of rolling is to warm and relax the tissue. Rolling encourages deep muscle relaxation.

CHUCKING

The chucking movement is accomplished by grasping the flesh firmly in one or both hands and moving it up and down along the bone. It is a series of quick movements along the axis of the limb.

WRINGING

Wringing is a back-and-forth movement in which the hands are placed a short distance apart on either side of the limb. It resembles wringing out a washcloth. The hands work in opposing directions, stretching and twisting the flesh against the bones in opposite directions. Your whole body is engaged in the movement. The hands make firm contact in both directions. Pressure is not so excessive as to cause pinching or burning (irritation) of the skin. Wringing gently stretches and warms the connective fascia.

SHAKING

Shaking is a movement that allows the recipient to release tension while indicating where he or she may be storing tension in a part of the body. The relaxed body part is gently yet forcefully shaken laterally or horizontally so that the relaxed flesh flops around the bone. You can observe where the body moves freely and where it seems to be stiff. Rigidness indicates body areas that are tense and require more attention. A type of bodywork known as Trager uses shaking and rocking extensively to locate and release tension. See Figure 2-11a through d.

JOSTLING

Jostling releases muscle tension, increases circulation, and relaxes muscles. It is most effective after muscles have exerted themselves, such as after a workout or competition. Jostling is done when the muscle is in a shortened and relaxed position. Grasp across the entire muscle, lift it slightly away from its position, and while the muscle remains relaxed, shake it quickly across its axis.

VIBRATION

Vibration is a continuous shaking or trembling movement transmitted from your hand and arm or from an electrical appliance to a fixed point, or along a selected area of the body. Vibration is often used to desensitize a point or area. Nerve trunks and centers are sometimes chosen as sites for the application of vibratory movements.

Manual contact vibration is usually done with the pads at the ends of the fingers or the soft touch of the palm of the hand. Light contact is made and the hand shaken back and forth as quickly as possible without moving over the skin where contact is being made.

The rate of vibration should be under your control. Manual vibrations usually range from 5 to 10 times per second, while mechanical vibrations can be adjusted to give from 10 to 100 vibrations per second. See Figure 2-12.

There are a variety of mechanical vibrators on the market that can be classified by size. A popular small model straps on the back of the hand.

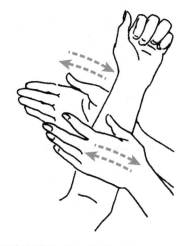

FIGURE 2-11a Rolling the arm.

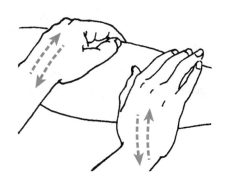

FIGURE 2-11b Wringing the muscles of the leg.

FIGURE 2-11c Chucking the arm.

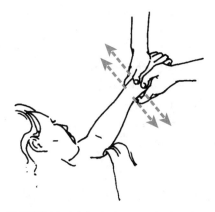

FIGURE 2-11d Shaking applied to the arm.

Another popular size is held (usually with two hands) and moved over the recipient's body. A larger floor-standing model unit uses a flexible applicator arm to deliver its therapeutic effects.

Another way to classify mechanical vibrators is by the vibrating action they use. An oscillating vibrator has a back-and-forth movement. An orbital vibrator uses a circular motion. These vibrators produce a shaking movement when applied to the body. Another type of vibrator produces

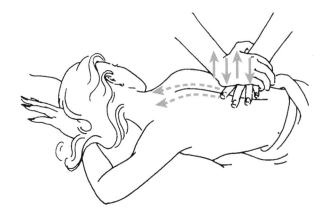

FIGURE 2-12 Vibrating over each vertebra.

"thumping" action. This rapid percussion/compression is directed into the tissues rather than laterally, along the surface. Using vibrators may enhance the effects of the massage and at the same time reduce your physical exertion.

The effect of vibratory movements depends on the rate of vibration, the intensity of pressure, and the duration of the treatment. This form of massage is soothing and brings about relaxation and release of tension when applied lightly. It is stimulating when applied with pressure. A numbing effect is experienced when vibrations are applied for a prolonged period of time.

PERCUSSION MOVEMENTS

Percussion movements include quick, striking manipulations such as tapping, beating, and slapping, which are highly stimulating to the body. Percussion movements are executed with both hands simultaneously or alternately. They do not use much force. Each blow to the body is a glancing contact during which your wrists remain very relaxed.

The general effects of percussion movements are to tone the muscles and impart a healthy glow to the part being massaged. With each striking movement, the muscles first contract and then relax as the fingers are removed from the body. In this way, muscles are toned. Percussion movements should never be applied over muscles that are abnormally contracted or over any sensitive area. See Figure 2-13a through e. The movements may be done in the following ways:

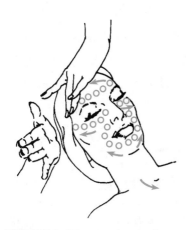

FIGURE 2-13a Tapping the face with the fingertips.

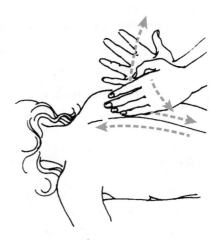

FIGURE 2-13b Hacking movements on the back.

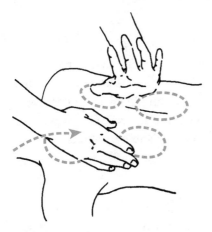

FIGURE 2-13c Slapping movements on the back.

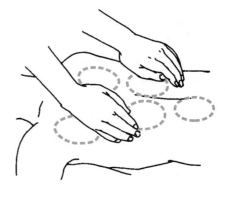

FIGURE 2-13d Cupping movements on the thorax.

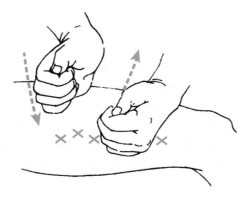

FIGURE 2-13e Beating the muscles of the thigh.

1. Tapping with tips of the fingers
2. Slapping with flattened palm and fingers of the hand
3. Cupping with the cupped palm of the hand
4. Hacking with the ulnar border of the hand
5. Beating with a softly clenched hand

TAPPING

Tapping or tapotement is the lightest, most superficial of the percussion techniques. Tapping is used over delicate, sensitive areas such as the face. Only the fingertips are used for tapping. The fingers may be slightly flexed so that only the tips make contact, or, with the fingers held relatively straight, the pads perform a very superficial slapping technique.

SLAPPING

Slapping is very stimulating and must be used sparingly. Slapping encourages peripheral circulation and creates a "glow" to the area. It is applied with the palmar surface of the fingers and the hand. As with all percussion strokes, the hands and wrists always remain loose and relaxed. Heavy pressure is avoided. Slapping uses a rhythmical, glancing contact with the body.

CUPPING

To perform cupping, form a cup by keeping the fingers together and slightly flexed and holding the thumb close to the side of the palm. On each percussion, the perimeter of the hand contacts the body. The resulting sound is a hollow popping.

HACKING

Hacking, much like vibration, encourages relaxation and local circulation. Some theories claim that hacking stimulates the nerve responses in muscles and helps to firm the muscles. Hacking is a rapid striking movement that can be done with one or both hands. When both hands are used the hands may strike alternately or together. A quick glancing strike is made with the little finger and the ulnar side of the hand. The wrist and fingers remain loose and relaxed and the fingers are slightly spread apart.

BEATING

Beating is the heaviest and deepest form of percussion and is done over the thicker, denser, and fleshier areas of the body. The hands are held in a loose fist. Contact is made with both hands, either together or alternately. The wrists are relaxed so the contact is the result of a rebounding, whip-like action of the hand and wrist. The force is never heavy or hard.

JOINT MOVEMENTS

There are a great variety of joint movements that can be used to manipulate any joint in the body, including joints of the toes, knees, hips, arms, or vertebrae, or even the less movable joints of the pelvis and cranium.

The basic classifications of joint movements are passive and active. Passive joint movements (PJM) are done while the recipient remains quietly relaxed and you stretch and move the part of the body to be exercised. Passive joint movements can be used as an assessment tool to determine normal movement (full range of movement without restriction or pain). Passive joint movements gently stretch the fibrous tissue and move the joint through its range of motion. PJMs are used therapeutically to improve joint mobility and range of motion.

When performing PJMs, hold and support the limb so the movement is directed toward the target joint. Move the limb in a normal movement pattern for that joint to the full extent of possible movement.

In active joint movements, the recipient actively participates in the exercise by contracting the muscles involved in the movement. For example, you would straighten the recipient's arm while asking him or her to hold against or resist the movement. Active joint movements may be subdivided into two categories: active resistive and active assistive.

Active assistive joint movements are a therapeutic technique to restore mobility in a limb that has been injured. They are used when the recipient is not able to move a limb or move it through a full range of motion. When performing active assistive joint movements, tell the recipient to make a specific movement. This is best done by moving the limb passively through the desired movement. As the recipient attempts the movement, assist the limb through that movement as necessary. The movement is repeated several times.

Active resistive joint movements refer to a number of therapeutic techniques that improve mobility, flexibility, or strength, depending on how the technique is performed. As the name indicates, active resistive joint movements involve a movement that the recipient makes while you resist it in some way. The type and degree of the movement, the extent and direction of the resistance, the duration of the resistance, and the sequence of the actions all have an effect on the outcome of the procedure.

To perform active resistive joint movements to shoulder flexion, instruct the recipient on the movement by passively moving the arm from a neutral position next to the side to a position high over the head. Instruct the recipient to repeat the movement on your command. Place one hand on the wrist and the other just above the elbow. Instruct the recipient to move the arm. Resist the recipient's movement but allow the movement to take place. Repeat the movement several times, resisting a little more each time but always allowing the full movement to take place. This type of movement builds strength in the specific muscle groups being challenged. Active resistive joint movements can target any specific muscle group in the body.

Joint movements are used to help restore the recipient's mobility or increase flexibility in a joint. Often, passive and active joint movements are combined. For example, to restore some mobility to a shoulder joint, instruct the recipient to raise the arm to the point of discomfort (active unassisted movement). Hold the arm in that position and tell the recipient to push against you and attempt to continue the movement (active resistive joint movement). Then tell the recipient to relax as you continue to move his or her arm (passive joint movement).

Joint movements may be applied with or without resistance, using either a forward, backward, or circular motion. To be most effective, joint movements should be applied through the full range of motion, which is the movement of a joint from one extreme of the articulation to the other. All joints have normal restrictions that limit the range of motion. Those restrictions may be bone to bone, such as the extension of the elbow where the movement is stopped when the olecronon of the ulna contacts the humerus. Sometimes the restriction is due to pull on ligaments as in the hyperextension of the hip. Most often it is due to muscles. As you passively move a joint to the end of its range, there is a sense that the limb is approaching the extent of its possible movement. The change in the quality of the feeling as the end of the movement is achieved is termed end feel. A hard end feel occurs when an abrupt clunk is felt at the end of the movement. This indicates that bone is making contact with another bone and stopping the movement. A soft end feel occurs when, over the last few inches or degrees of the joint movement, there is a gradual and steady tightening until a soft barrier is reached. Soft tissue limits the range in a soft end feel.

Ideally every joint should move through its full range of motion freely, without discomfort. Often the range of motion is further restricted by tense muscles, injured or restricted tissues, inflammation, or other pathological conditions. The reaction of joint movements with these conditions is usually pain. Be aware of the end feel of the joints and the pain reactions of the recipient when doing joint movements. Joint movements have a great therapeutic benefit as an assessment tool and as a treatment to enhance function and mobility. See Figure 2-14a through j.

FIGURE 2-14a Apply joint movements and rotation. Note the interlacing of the fingers.

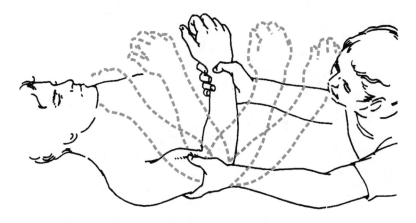

FIGURE 2-14b Flexion and extension of the forearm.

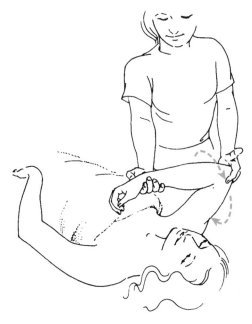

FIGURE 2-14c Rotate the shoulder.

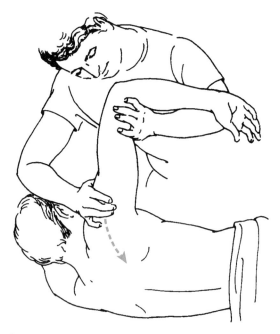

FIGURE 2-14d Abduction of the arm. This is movement of a part away from the median line of the body.

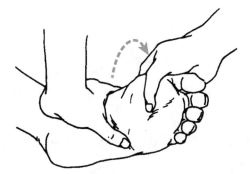

FIGURE 2-14e Rotate and stretch the tarsals and metatarsals.

FIGURE 2-14f Circumduction of the thigh.

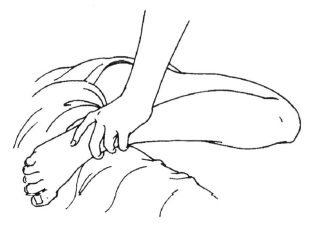

FIGURE 2-14g Apply joint movement.

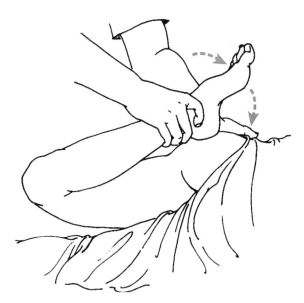

FIGURE 2-14h Flex the recipient's knee, pressing the heel against the gluteals.

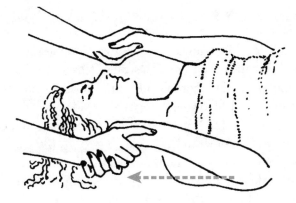

FIGURE 2-14i Active movement: The recipient tries to move her hands above her head as you resist or assist.

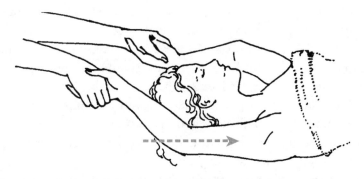

FIGURE 2-14j Active movement: The recipient attempts to bring her arms back down to her sides as you resist the movement.

RHYTHM AND PRESSURE IN MASSAGE

People have individual vibrations and their own sense of rhythm. You need to remember that some people are high strung (tense), while others are very low key (relaxed). It is important to work with people according to their particular needs instead of following a personal agenda and possibly working against their natural rhythm. The rhythm must be steady and slightly slower than the client's pace in order to have a sedating effect. If the massage is part of an athletic training program, however, the rhythm may be more upbeat. You can develop skills to tune in to other people and work more effectively with them as individuals.

Breathing is a part of the body's natural rhythm and is important to your stamina and ability to move easily while giving massage.

You must develop an awareness of the right amount of pressure to be used for various therapeutic situations and techniques. It is important to begin to massage in an area of the body cautiously, gently, and lightly and then to apply more pressure as you become aware of underlying structures and the condition of tissues. This also helps you to note tension and stress build-up and determine how to proceed according to the recipient's body condition and sensitivity. The pressure varies with the technique used and according to the intended outcome. At no time should the pressure be so forceful as to cause injury to the tissues. The rule is to begin with a light and sensitive touch, and increase the pressure as you work into an area. As tension in the area begins to dissipate and the muscles relax, the recipient will let you in even deeper. When it is time to leave the area, back out gradually, smoothing the way as you go.

One of the primary indications of tension or dysfunction in the muscles and soft tissue is pain. People have different tolerances for pain, and it is important not to produce so much pain that the individual's pain threshold is crossed. When that happens, the recipient will tense up and the work will become less effective.

Complete Body Massage

The following step-by-step procedure helps you to learn basic massage techniques quickly.

GENERAL ARM MASSAGE

1. Raise the person's arm.
2. Stroke the arm three times.
3. Knead the arm from the shoulder to the elbow.
4. Stroke the arm from the elbow to the shoulder.
5. Bend the elbow and rest it on the table.
6. Knead the arm from the elbow to the wrist.
7. Stroke the arm from the wrist to the elbow.
8. Press the metacarpal bones back and forth.
9. Knead each finger and hand.
10. Rotate each finger.
11. Stroke the arm.
12. Roll the arm three times.
13. Apply joint movements to the arm.
14. Stroke the arm lightly three times.
15. Apply nerve strokes.

Arm Movements for Body Massage

The following movements may be included or omitted. See Figure 3-1a through p.

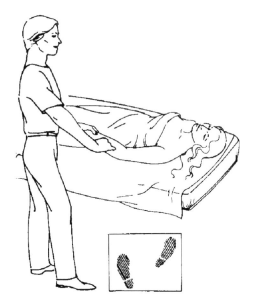

FIGURE 3-1a Proper stance and posture are important. Proper posture reduces fatigue, and proper stance allows mobility and power.

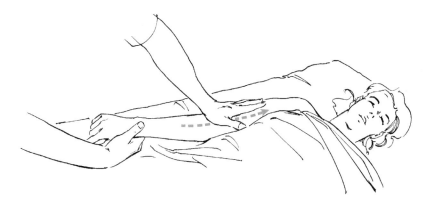

FIGURE 3-1b Stroke the arm from the hand to the shoulder.

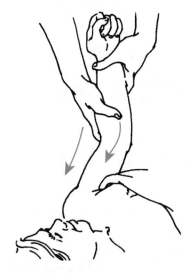

FIGURE 3-1c Direction of effleurage and position of arm. The same upward movement is applied when massaging the back of the arm.

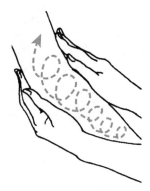

FIGURE 3-1d Circular kneading of the arm

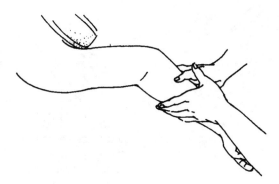

FIGURE 3-1e Continue petrissage down the arm to the wrist.

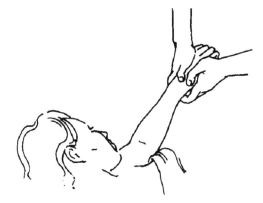

FIGURE 3-1f Knead the carpals and metacarpals.

FIGURE 3-1g Circular kneading of the fingers and hand

FIGURE 3-1h While holding the hand, massage the palm, back of the hand, metacarpals, fingers, and upward over the wrist.

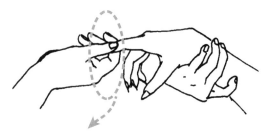

FIGURE 3-1i Hold the forearm firmly. Rotate and circumduct the wrist. Knead and rotate each finger as you circumduct and apply traction.

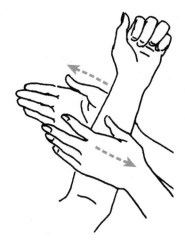

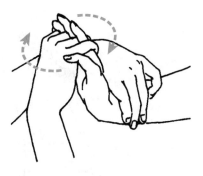

FIGURE 3-1k Apply joint movements and rotation. Note the interlacing of the fingers.

FIGURE 3-1j Roll the arm.

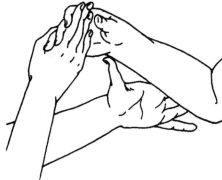

FIGURE 3-1l Rotate the forearm. Note how the fingers are used to steady the elbow.

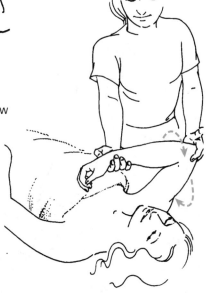

FIGURE 3-1m Rotate the shoulder by moving the elbow. Note how the other hand supports the hand.

FIGURE 3-1n Abduction of the arm. This is a movement of a part away from the median line of the body.

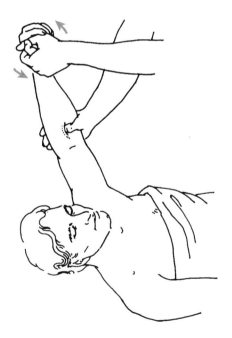

FIGURE 3-1o Circumduction of the arm

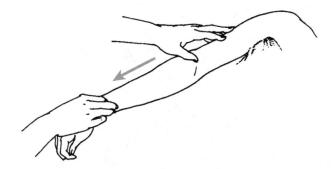

FIGURE 3-1p Apply feather strokes (light effleurage) with your fingertips to complete the massage of the arm. The massage for the other arm is done in the same sequence of movements.

GENERAL MASSAGE FOR THE FOOT AND LEG

1. Stroke the leg three times.
2. Press metatarsal bones of the foot back and forth.
3. Knead each toe, around foot, and ankle.
4. Rotate each toe three times.
5. Knead the leg three times.
6. Wring and roll the leg.
7. Stroke the leg three times.
8. Apply joint movements to the leg.
9. Stroke the leg lightly three times.
10. Apply nerve strokes to the leg.

Massage for the Foot and Leg

The following movements may be included or omitted. See Figures 3-2 and 3-3a through r.

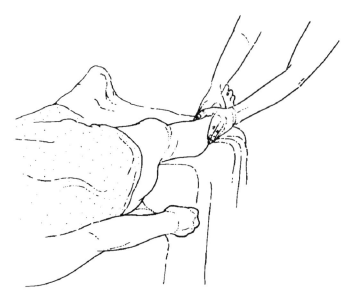

FIGURE 3-2 Stroke the leg in long movements from the ankle to the hip. Apply more pressure on the stroke up the leg, and maintain light contact as your hands glide back to the starting point.

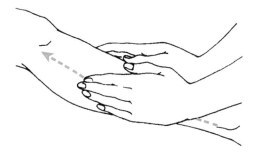

FIGURE 3-3a Apply pressure on the stroke in the direction of venous blood and lymph flow.

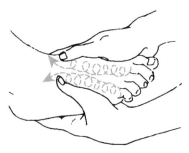

FIGURE 3-3b Circular kneading of the foot

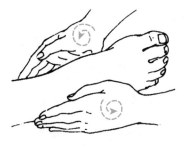

FIGURE 3-3c Warm the foot and ankles with circular rubbing movements.

FIGURE 3-3d Apply digital friction between the tendons and bones on all surfaces of the foot.

FIGURE 3-3e Massage and rotate each digit.

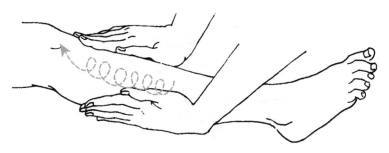

FIGURE 3-3f Circular kneading of the leg and thigh

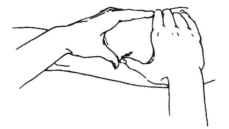

FIGURE 3-3g Apply petrissage to the anterior leg.

FIGURE 3-3h Apply fulling (compression) movements.

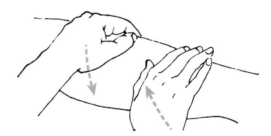

FIGURE 3-3i Wring the muscles of the thigh.

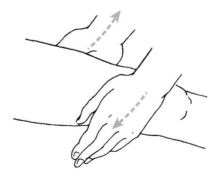

FIGURE 3-3j Roll the muscles of the thigh.

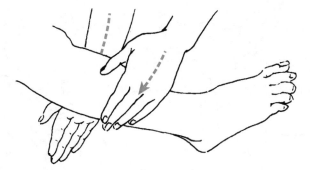

FIGURE 3-3k Roll the muscles of the leg.

FIGURE 3-3l Stretch the plantar surface of the foot and toes.

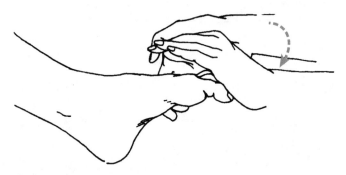

FIGURE 3-3m Stretch the dorsal aspect of the foot and toes.

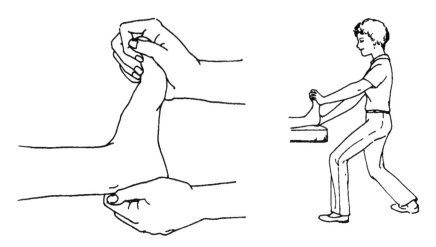

FIGURE 3-3n Stretch the Achilles' tendon. Note the position of the hands.

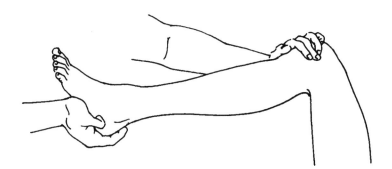

FIGURE 3-3o Apply joint movements. The knee may be moved all the way to the chest, or this position may be used for joint rotations of the hip and knee in the range of motion. Note the position of the hands at the heel and knee.

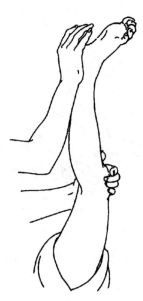

FIGURE 3-3p Apply hamstring stretching movements.

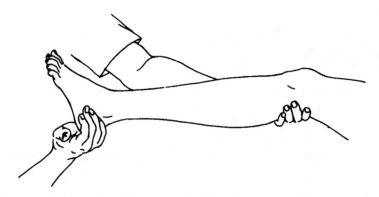

FIGURE 3-3q Continue the stretching movements. Note how the hand is placed to support under the knee to avoid hyperextension of the leg.

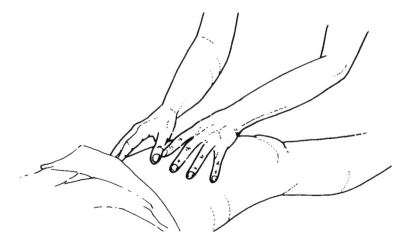

FIGURE 3-3r Complete the massage of the leg with a nerve stroke.

GENERAL MASSAGE FOR THE CHEST AND NECK

1. From the head of the table, stroke the back of the neck.
2. Knead the back and sides of the neck and shoulders.
3. Stroke the chest three times. Stroke down the chest, around to the sides, coming up under each arm, and up and over the shoulders to the neck.
4. Apply deep gliding strokes along the ribs from the table toward the center of the chest.
5. Apply kneading to the pectoral muscles. (Avoid breast tissue on women.)
6. Repeat step #3.

Chest and Neck Movements

The following movements may be included or omitted. See Figure 3-4a through h.

FIGURE 3-4a Apply effleurage from the sternal notch, over the shoulders, and along the trapezius.

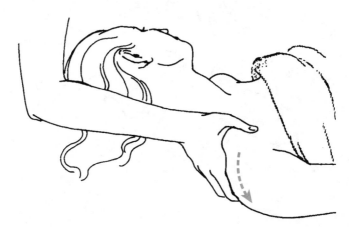

FIGURE 3-4b Continue the movement across the shoulder and around the deltoid.

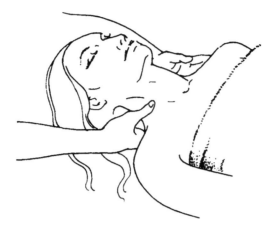

FIGURE 3-4c Continue the movement up to the occipital ridge.

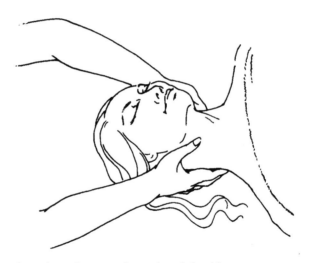

FIGURE 3-4d Apply petrissage to the neck and shoulders.

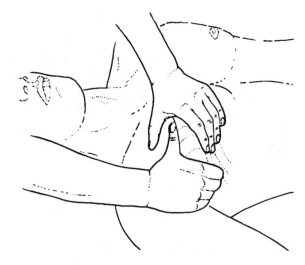

FIGURE 3-4e Kneading and friction to the pectoral muscles.

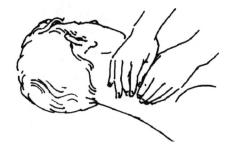

FIGURE 3-4f Petrissage to back of neck and shoulder region.

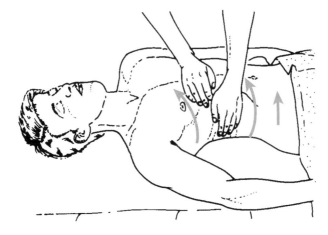

FIGURE 3-4g Alternate hand stroking (shingles) is applied from the axillary area to the hips.

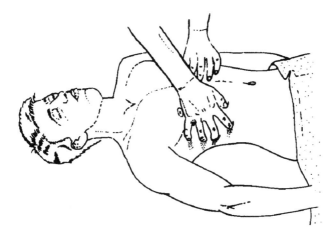

FIGURE 3-4h Raking is done by flexing the tips of the fingers and stroking along the ribs from the table to the midline of the body.

GENERAL MASSAGE MOVEMENTS FOR THE ABDOMEN

1. Stroke around the abdominal area in a clockwise direction three times.
2. Knead the abdominal muscles back and forth three times.
3. Vibrate the abdominal area with a circular motion over colon, intestines, stomach, and liver.
4. Stroke the abdomen lightly three times.

Abdominal Movements for Body Massage

The following movements may be included or omitted. See Figure 3-5a through d.

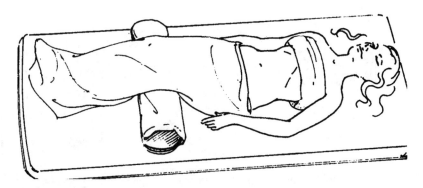

FIGURE 3-5a This is the correct position and draping for massage of the abdomen. Oil is applied before beginning the massage. A folded towel is used to cover the female recipient's breasts. A bolster may be used to support the knees.

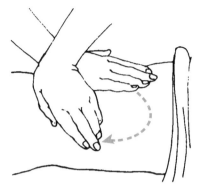

FIGURE 3-5b Stroking the abdomen with deep circular movement.

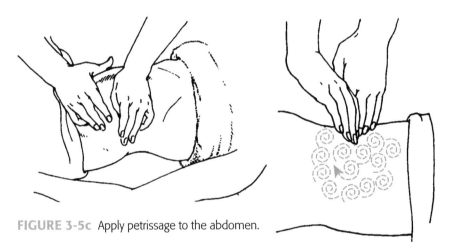

FIGURE 3-5c Apply petrissage to the abdomen.

FIGURE 3-5d Apply circular friction following the tract of the large intestine.

CHANGING POSITION

Have the person receiving the massage turn over to a prone, facedownward position.

GENERAL MASSAGE FOR THE BACK OF THE LEGS

1. Apply oil to leg.
2. Move legs apart and stroke leg three times.
3. Knead foot from toe to heel.
4. Knead leg from the heels to the hips.
5. Apply wringing and rolling.
6. Stroke each leg three times.
7. Apply nerve strokes.

Back of Leg Movements for Body Massage

The following movements may be included or omitted. See Figure 3-6a through g.

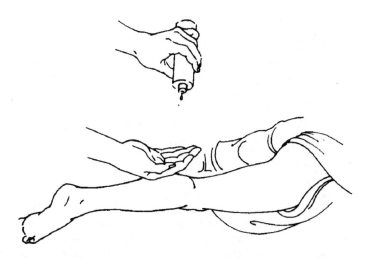

FIGURE 3-6a Before beginning massage movements, prepare the posterior leg by draping and applying oil.

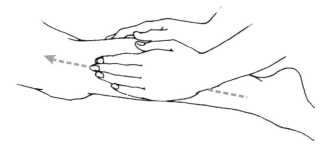

FIGURE 3-6b Stroke the leg upward with both hands.

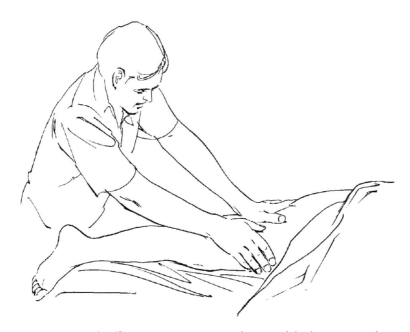

FIGURE 3-6c Apply effleurage movements. Stroke toward the heart. Note: The leading hand is on the lateral aspect of the leg in order to travel up and over the gluteal muscles and the iliac crest and back down the lateral side of the leg. At the same time, the medial hand travels up to the gluteal crease and back down the medial side of the leg. Both hands return to the starting point to repeat the stroke three or more times.

FIGURE 3-6d Knead the calf muscles.

FIGURE 3-6e Apply fulling or compression strokes to the entire leg.

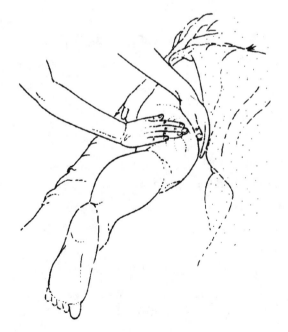

FIGURE 3-6f Apply wringing to the back of the leg.

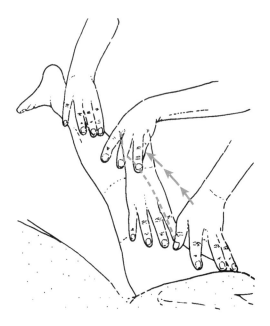

FIGURE 3-6g Complete the massage of the posterior leg with several feather strokes (nerve stroke) from the hip to the foot.

GENERAL MASSAGE FOR THE BACK OF THE BODY

1. Apply oil to the back.
2. Stroke the back five times up the spine and down on each side of the body.
3. Place the hands flat on each side of the spine and stretch them outward toward the shoulders.
4. Continue step 2 to cover the entire back.
5. Vibrate along each side of the vertebral column from the neck to the sacrum.
6. Knead the entire back and each side of the torso.
7. Apply deep gliding strokes from the table to the center of the back (shingles) and from the hips to the shoulders.

8. From the head of the table, stroke the back three times. From the back of the neck, stroke down along the length of the spine, around to the side of the body, up the sides, around and over the shoulders, up to the neck, and repeat.

9. Apply light hacking movements along the spine, between the shoulders, over the gluteal muscles, and on the back of the legs. Avoid the kidney area.

10. Stroke the back lightly five times.

11. Apply nerve strokes to the entire back and complete the massage.

Back Movements for Body Massage

The following movements may be included or omitted. See Figure 3-7a through l.

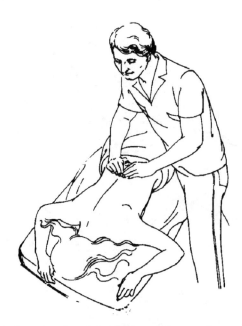

FIGURE 3-7a Begin at the gluteal cleft and apply long strokes up along the muscles on each side of the spine.

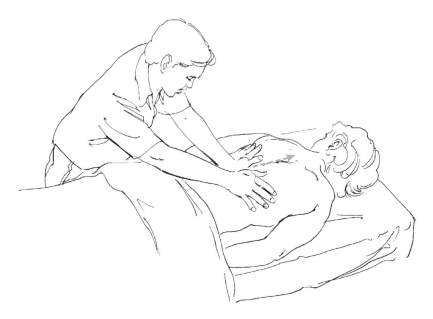

FIGURE 3-7b Continue with effleurage strokes up the back and over the shoulders.

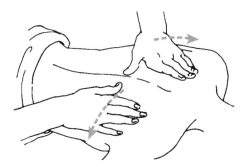

FIGURE 3-7c Outward stretching of the muscles of the back

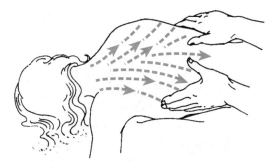

FIGURE 3-7d Fan stroking of the back

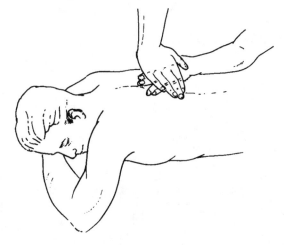

FIGURE 3-7e Vibration movements are applied over each vertebra by placing the fingers of one hand on each side of the spinous process and the other hand on top. Vibrate back and forth as you move down along the spine.

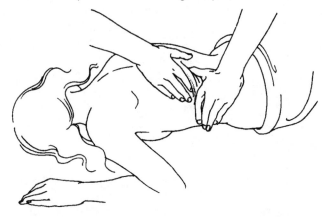

FIGURE 3-7f Apply petrissage to the entire side that is opposite you. This takes several passes.

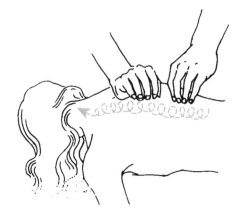

FIGURE 3-7g Kneading around the spine

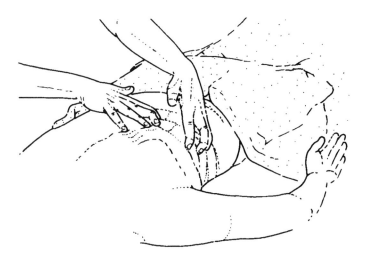

FIGURE 3-7h Raking is applied in alternate strokes so the tips of the fingers glide between the ribs.

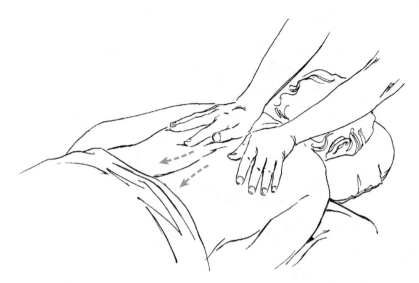

FIGURE 3-7i Continue effleurage movements down the back, over and around the gluteal muscles, back up the sides, then over and around the shoulders to the nape of the neck.

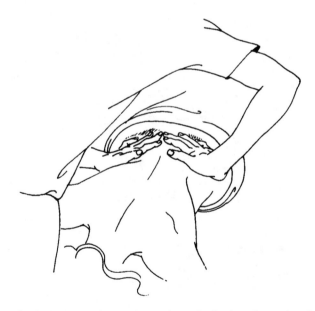

FIGURE 3-7j The caring stroke continues down the back and over the gluteal muscles.

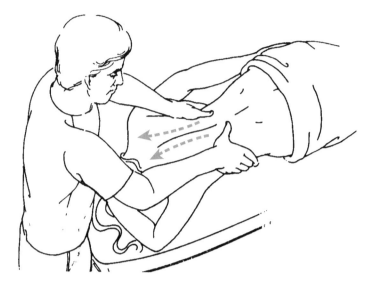

FIGURE 3-7k The caring stroke is a continuous movement that proceeds up the side and around the shoulder to return to the starting point.

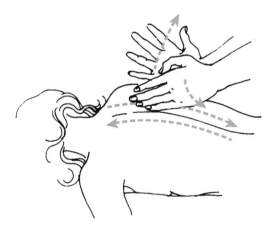

FIGURE 3-7l Hacking movements on the back

Shiatsu Massage

Research has shown in numerous cases the impact that touch has on the body—how some children who were held and nurtured by their mothers while still infants grow up to be more stable than children who were left in hospital nurseries. Research tells of certain animals who survive after birth only if the mother immediately licks off the baby. Animals that weren't licked off often died of some kind of internal functional failure. Hence, the impact of tactile stimulation may be a fundamental and essential ingredient of life that we have yet to fully understand. We do know that it seems to be a part of the healthy development of every kind of organism.

The entire concept of *Shiatsu* is the idea of Shi (finger) and atsu (pressure), a massage therapy in which pressure from the fingers and hands is applied to the body of the recipient. Just the touch of the fingers to skin causes differing degrees of sensation. All sensations first sensed in the skin are transferred back to the brain for action by the nervous system. Such a complex organ deserves very careful handling.

Shiatsu is quite simple to do once you are knowledgeable and experienced. For the novice, however, it takes serious concentration and focus to perform the treatment on this highly sensitive tactile organ effectively, all the while developing a more sensitive sense of touch and point of reference. It is important, in mastering the art of *Shiatsu,* to be cognizant from the start of the inherent and dramatic effect touch has on you and the recipient. It is an art that takes focus, concentration, and practice to do well.

THE HANDS

Take a close look at the inside of your hands and study the contours of your fingers. You'll note an elevated tip on each finger and thumb. These elevated pads appear to have the greatest tactile sensitivity, and lend themselves to effective *Shiatsu* massage. Although the palms of the hands are also used to perform *Shiatsu,* the primary tools are the thumbs and fingers.

The tips of the fingers should never be used for *Shiatsu,* although there are some in the field who would disagree. The weight and pressure for application must emanate from your body through the first pads of the thumbs and fingers. Pressure should also not be applied at the point between the first and second joint of the thumbs or fingers. Using the tips or joints can radically change the quality of the massage and the comfort of the recipient and can cause carpal tunnel syndrome and other ailments in you.

As much as possible, the pressure should emanate from the position and movement of your body. This not only balances and keeps the pressure more even from the recipient's standpoint but also takes the stress and strain off your hands. Several different positions of the hands and fingers are available for use according to the area. The most common follow.

Proper Use of Hands and Fingers

THUMBS

Thumbs are ideal for parts of the body where concentrated pressure is desired, such as the temples, the tops of the shoulders, along the spine, and the center of the calves. Thumbs can be used side by side, one at a time, or overlapped for greater pressure. When using thumbs, it's important to have the other four fingers spread to the side for added support. Sometimes the thumb and first or second finger are used together such as when doing the toes or fingers.

FINGERS

You may choose to use just the first and middle finger, the first three fingers, all four fingers, or just one finger depending on the area. Remember, use the first pad, not the fingertips. The index finger tends to have rather strong pressure and may be too strong on sensitive facial areas unless all fingers are used. The counterbalance of several fingers helps prevent too much pressure from just one. Sometimes greater pressure can be achieved when the middle finger overlaps the index finger. The choice of finger combinations will come naturally with practice.

PALMS OR FULL HANDS

These are often used on larger areas. For example, full hands are used to cover the whole face at one time. Palms by themselves are helpful on the lower back and upper buttocks. Sometimes you will use either the inner palm (next to the thumb) or the outer palm (next to the little finger) for stronger concentration. When greater pressure is desired, hands may also overlap as with fingers. Overlapping palms also give a stabilizing effect on the back, shoulders, or head. Even though it would seem that overlapping hands or palms would make the pressure overly strong, with balance it often softens the pressure while adding depth. Full hands and palms are very useful in full body *Shiatsu* treatments.

APPLICATION OF PRESSURE

The key to successful treatment is the ability to apply the correct amount of pressure to the area being treated. It should never be painful to the recipient. If the pressure exerted is so strong as to be painful, the application is incorrect.

There is, however, a fine line between pleasant discomfort and pain. It's difficult to describe the proper pressure because it varies widely from area to area and person to person. In reality, where there is acute pain, it may be indicative of a reflex or corresponding problem somewhere else along the meridian system or in a corresponding organ.

However, since we are not using *Shiatsu* to cure ailments, the mere fact that there is pain should only help us to understand better and perhaps relieve that pain coincidentally while relaxing the area of discomfort. Our goal is to relieve fatigue and stress and improve metabolism and circulation, so overly heavy pressure is not part of our treatment and is completely unnecessary for the goal we have in mind. However, if the discomfort is related to a buildup of lactic acid in the muscle or area, then it's very effective for relieving this condition and the discomfort is normal to a minor degree.

Heavier pressure may be used as long as the recipient is not hurting. "Comfortable pain" is the operative word. It is difficult to explain what is meant by comfortable pain. Flossing your teeth hurts a bit, but it feels good because you know you're getting the teeth clean. You want just enough pressure to know something is happening but not enough to cause pain. Also, pressure sustained for too long can cause the muscles to tense up, which is the opposite of our goal of relaxation. Hence, mild pressure for short periods of time works best in esthetic treatments. If there is an area you feel you would like to concentrate on, then apply pressure, move to another area, and come back again. It is strongly recommended that in addition to this book you obtain videos and attend hands-on classes to better learn the movements, the pressures to be applied, and rhythm.

Depth and Duration of Pressure

At the beginning of a massage, as pressure is applied to the first few areas, the recipient should be asked how the pressure is. If it is comfortable, proceed at that rate. It is prudent to ask periodically if the recipient is awake. If the person has gone to sleep, keep the pressure level about the same.

The duration of pressure also depends somewhat on the recipient, but normally most areas of the body should be pressed for approximately ten seconds per point. A particularly distressed area may require a little more or a little less. An excellent method for timing the length and depth of pressure is to inhale when you touch and slowly exhale as you apply the pressure. It is imperative to effective *Shiatsu* that you not rush. Slow, even, rhythmic movements are most effective. As you are first learning, it is wise to verbalize the following count exactly to develop good timing: Touch on 1, press on 2, release on 3.

Don't shorten the words, and say each line evenly. This will equate to approximately ten seconds, but you must do this out loud as you are practicing the pressure. It's almost impossible to apply the correct amount of pressure for the right amount of time if you are trying to carry on a conversation. It's imperative that you quietly concentrate. Keep in mind also that you must try to balance the left and right hand pressure as closely as possible, unless you're concentrating on a specific point.

Pressure and *Tsubo* Location

There are thought to be more than one thousand *Tsubo* or motor points in the body, but there are only about 365 that we deal with directly in *Shiatsu*. Even at that you cannot possibly locate each point on every person. Additionally, even common *Tsubo* may be located in slightly different areas on each individual. This is why practice is the key to effective *Shiatsu* treatment. The *Tsubo* may be located in the following ways:

1. As a natural dent or hollow in the skin such as the temples or between the joints of the fingers. The common areas of dents normally indicate healthy energy flow and locating the point is relatively easy. These areas are not overly sensitive to average pressure.

2. As a lump or bump similar to the "golf balls" we often find when massaging someone's shoulders. These bumps may be indicative of lactic acid buildup or a blockage of the energy, and even slight pressure may be quite uncomfortable. Light and repeated pressure is recommended here.

3. As shown on general anatomy charts or diagrams. Since you are not learning *Shiatsu* for medical application, exact location of a specific *Tsubo* is not critical to the success of the overall area treatment. General application still increases circulation, improves metabolism and overall well-being, and relaxes.

The beginning student of *Shiatsu* will certainly have difficulty discerning dents and bumps, but it's exciting to develop better perception. A good practice is to just glide your thumbs or fingers up and down the arm feeling the lumpiness between the muscles. Another very lumpy area is the head, if you can find a bald person or someone with short light hair who will allow you to practice. Do not feel frustrated in the beginning; this will come naturally as you become more familiar with the practice.

Caution in Pressure

Shiatsu can be done on almost anyone, even after a recent face-lift where the skin should not be rubbed or massaged. However, the amount of pressure must be considered. There are very few contraindications to *Shiatsu* and common sense will normally advise you when not to use it. But as a reminder, do not do *Shiatsu* on the following:

1. Varicose veins, couperose, distended capillaries, or any other vascular disorder.

2. Abdominal areas during pregnancy, disease, or discomfort.

3. Anyone with a disease where pressure could be a problem.

4. Areas of open wounds, lesions, inflammation, infection, edema.

5. Anyone in a situation you feel is questionable. (Have the recipient consult a physician prior to performing *Shiatsu.*)

And finally, any time there is question about the amount of pressure to be applied, just lighten the pressure to the touch level.

IMPORTANCE OF RELAXATION

Concentration is critical to developing the tactile sensory ability to locate *Tsubo,* but it's imperative that you also be relaxed. If you are stressed or in a hurry, you will not only have more difficulty finding the *Tsubo* but you will also have great difficulty in balancing your rhythm and pressure. *Shiatsu* is not something that can be done in a rush. If you relax and have the right atmosphere, perhaps some quiet soft music, you will easily develop a smooth natural rhythm and will breathe correctly as you perform the pressure in each location. Many experts in *Shiatsu* also study yoga, relaxation, and meditation techniques, not from a spiritual or religious standpoint but to improve on the actual application of *Shiatsu* for optimum results.

In addition to mental relaxation, it's also good to perform warm-up exercises for the thumbs, fingers, and hands to relax and limber up. The more relaxed your hands are, the easier it is to remember that all pressure should come from your body weight, not your hands. Tight, tense hands will fatigue easily and will also not be as effective at detecting sensory conditions.

Performing *Shiatsu*

HEAD AND SCALP

Purpose

1. Stimulates circulation and subsequent nutrition to the scalp and hair roots, which promotes good healthy hair growth

2. Relieves stress and tension

3. Relaxes hair follicles allowing better absorption of conditioning agents

4. Helps stimulate sebaceous gland production to lubricate dry hair and improve the condition

Technique

This treatment can be done on a wet or dry head. Before beginning the *Shiatsu* be sure to massage the entire head with the fingertips.

1. Press the main *Tsubo* at the crown of the head three times.

2. Move to the front of the forehead at the hairline. Apply pressure to three points about one-half inch apart from the center line to the top of the ear on the left side and then the right.

3. Move back about one-half inch to the next row of *Tsubo* and repeat left, then right. Repeat row after row until you reach the main crown point. On most heads you will have five rows from the forehead to the crown.

4. Depending on the position of the client, you may need to use one hand to brace the head from the forehead and the other thumb and your body weight to press in toward the face on the back side of the head. There should be three points on each side of the

center line on the left side and then the right. Each row should also be about one-half inch apart. You should have about five rows from the crown to the base of the head.

5. The last row for the base of the head should be just under the occipital. Place all four fingers cradling the head, and this time your pressure should be applied with a lifting movement as if you would lift the head off the neck.

6. Apply pressure with thumbs to the temples.

7. Using the four fingers and thumb in a vice-like grip, apply pressure in three straight rows down the neck to the shoulders. The first time the four fingers of the right hand will be on the right-hand side of the neck. The second time switch hands and the four fingers of the left hand will be on the left-hand side of the neck.

8. Massage upper shoulders and apply pressure to *Tsubo* on the upper area of the shoulders as desired. Normally apply pressure to about three points on top of each shoulder.

End the *Shiatsu* with relaxing massage of the entire head, neck, and shoulders.

FULL FACIAL SHIATSU

Purpose

1. Stimulates circulation without moving skin. If done without premassage, may help stimulate natural healing for post-facial cosmetic surgical procedure (face-lift).

2. Relaxes the facial features, thus reducing fatigue.

3. Increases nutritional exchanges and enhances absorption of products.

4. Relieves stress.

5. Relaxes facial muscles.

6. Helps even out skin tones.

7. Feels great and relaxes.

8. Indirectly improves all functions of the skin and body in the area treated.

9. Pressure around the eyes relieves fatigue, dryness, redness, and itchiness.

10. Pressure on the temples relieves stress and may help relieve tension.

11. Pressure in the sinus group will relieve pressure buildup, assist in decongesting the sinuses, and relieve pressure to the eye and forehead areas.

12. Pressure around the mouth helps freshen breath.

13. Pressure on the cheeks relieves stress and tension and relaxes the face, particularly for someone who talks a lot.

Imagine the face, neck, and chest divided into two sections with about three rows in each section (some people have only two rows and some have four). Movements are normally done from the center of the face or body outward and from the top of the head downward. Both sides of the face and chest will be done simultaneously so even, balanced pressure is required.

1. Using the first four fingers, start applying pressure at the upper row right at the hairline. See Figure 5-1. Do three rows from the center of the forehead out to the top of the ears. Use middle and ring fingers or thumbs to apply pressure to the temples. See Figure 5-2.

2. Slide to about the middle of the forehead, repeat with three rows out to the top of the ear, and repeat temples as desired.

3. The last forehead row should be right on top of the eyebrows. Repeat three rows. Repeat temples as desired.

4. Apply pressure with middle or ring finger to upper inner corner of eye just inside and under ocular bone. See Figure 5-3.

5. Move to middle of upper eye; repeat pressure with same finger. See Figure 5-4.

6. Move to outer corner of eye at junction of upper and lower eyelid; repeat pressure with same finger. See Figure 5-5.

7. Apply pressure to temples with fingers or thumbs. See Figure 5-6.

8. Repeat upper inner corner eye point.

9. Move to lower inner corner of eye at tear duct; apply lighter pressure with finger.

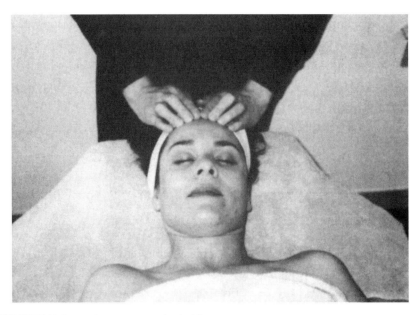

FIGURE 5-1 Apply pressure at the hairline.

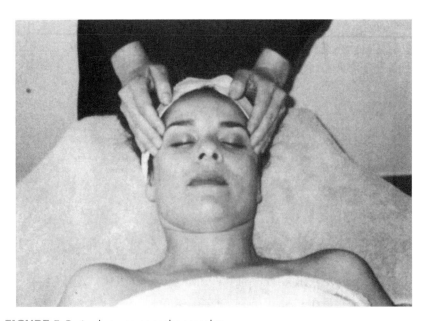

FIGURE 5-2 Apply pressure to the temples.

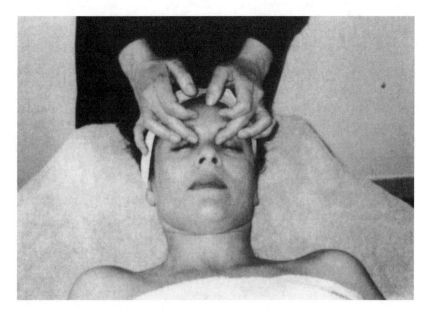

FIGURE 5-3 Apply pressure to the inner corner of the eye.

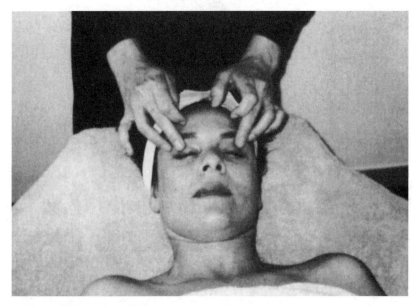

FIGURE 5-4 Apply pressure to the middle of the eye.

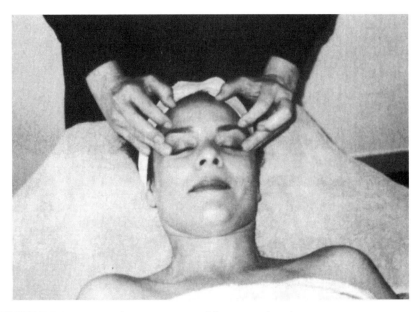

FIGURE 5-5 Move to the outer corner of the eye and apply pressure.

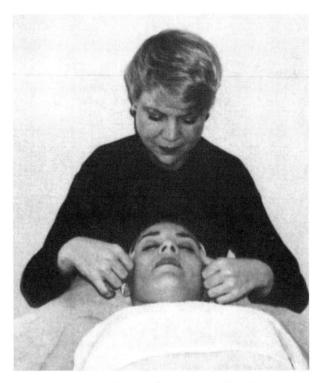

FIGURE 5-6 Apply pressure at the temples, using the thumbs.

10. Move to lower middle of eye; apply light pressure with same finger.

11. Move to outer corner of eye (same location as outer corner when doing upper eye); apply pressure.

12. Repeat temples.

13. Repeat upper inner corner of eye.

14. Move to upper sinus area just below tear duct. Apply pressure with same finger. See Figure 5-7.

15. Move slightly down and out to main sinus *Tsubo* and apply pressure. See Figure 5-8.

16. Move to just under nostrils (deep dent) and apply pressure without blocking nostrils or applying pressure in toward nostrils.

NOTE! *All three points for sinus are to be done on the face, not in or on the nose itself.*

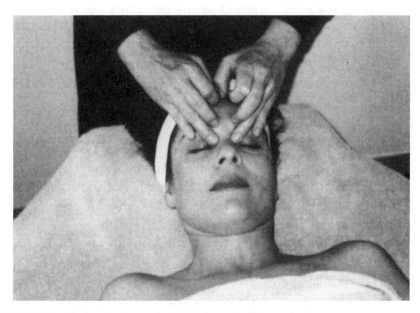

FIGURE 5-7 Move to the upper sinus area and apply pressure.

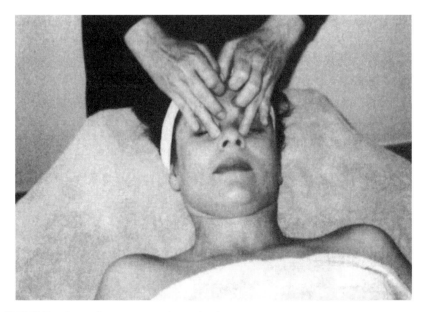

FIGURE 5-8 Apply pressure to the main sinus area.

17. The upper lip area is to be done in a slightly lifting movement to be sure that pressure is applied directly to the gums, not the teeth. Four fingers may be used to apply direct pressure. If the area is small or your fingers appear to be too large, apply pressure with the sides of the middle or ring fingers covering the entire upper lip area. See Figure 5-9.

18. The lower lip area should be done in the same manner, either with direct finger pressure or sides of fingers in a slightly downward pressure to be sure the pressure is on the gums.

19. Move back up to the middle sinus point for finger placement reference. Using three or four fingers, apply pressure in three rows from that point directly on the cheeks out to the top of the ear. See Figure 5-10.

20. Move down to the last sinus point under the nostrils to begin the middle cheek row. This row requires that the fingers lift up under the muscles in three rows out to the middle flap of the ear.

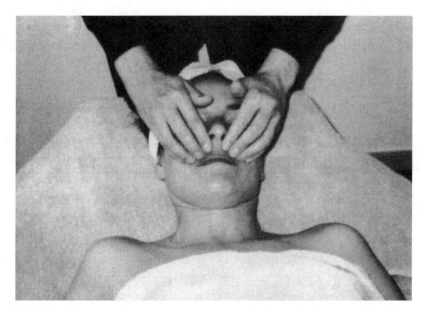

FIGURE 5-9 Use fingers to apply pressure to the entire upper lip area.

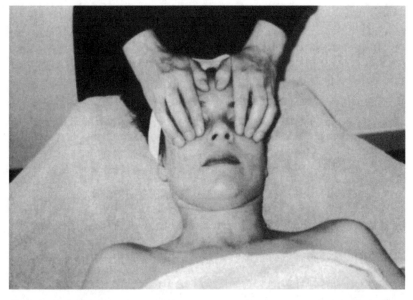

FIGURE 5-10 Apply pressure in three rows from that point directly on the cheeks out to the tops of the ears.

21. The last row will be done with four fingers starting on top of the center of the chin and working out in three rows to the base of the ears. Figure 5-11.

22. The ear group will be done in two rows, one on the outer cartilage of the ear and the second on the inner heavier cartilage of the ear. There will be approximately eight points very close together moving from the earlobe up and around to the top of the ear and then the ear flap. Pressure will be applied with thumb and first finger up and around with equal pressure on both sides. See Figure 5-12. The inner row will be with pressure mostly from the thumbs only while the fingers support the ears.

23. Apply full two hands pressure for the entire face. Placement of hands is flat on the face facing downward with the pads of the palms resting on the eyebrows. Hands do not cover the nose. Apply full even hand pressure and then open hands as if opening a book. Close hands and repeat pressure and opening technique three times.

24. The front sides of the neck are optional. Pressure is applied just next to the esophagus on the platysma muscle with very light four finger pressure. See Figure 5-13. Three rows may be done

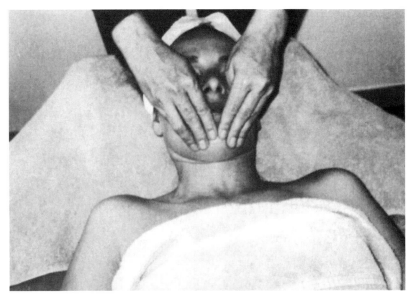

FIGURE 5-11 Using four fingers, apply pressure to the center of the chin.

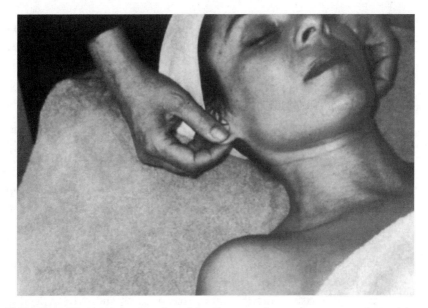

FIGURE 5-12 Using the thumb and first finger, apply equal pressure to the earlobes.

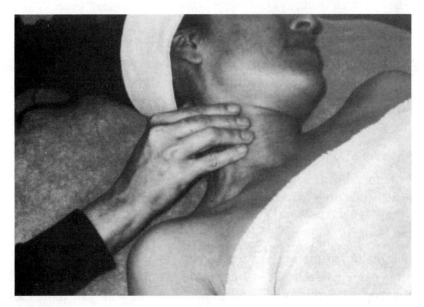

FIGURE 5-13 Using four fingers, apply light pressure just next to the esophagus on the platysma muscle.

from the top of the neck to the base of the neck as long as no pressure is applied in the area of the lymph nodes on the neck just above the clavicle.

25. Apply direct four finger pressure in toward the center of the neck on the sides just behind the ears down to the base of the neck.

26. Apply thumb pressure to three *Tsubo* on top of shoulders and then on the center point at the top of the arm (top of deltoid muscle).

27. There will be approximately three rows for the chest from the top of the clavicle on both sides of the sternum between the ribs to the beginning of the breasts. No pressure is applied to the breasts themselves. Beginning just to the sides of the sternum apply full four finger pressure to approximately three rows out to the arm joint. Be sure the last row as you move down follows a line to the axilla. The last points are particularly relaxing and stress relieving. Do not apply pressure to lymph nodes in axilla area.

28. Final pressure on the chest will be done sideways with full hands on both sides of the sternum in a manner similar to that done with the hands on the face.

The full facial treatment ends with a closing effleurage massage.

EYE TREATMENT

Purpose

1. Relieves eye fatigue
2. Helps eyes lubricate and self-clarify (reduces redness)
3. Relaxes eyes to improve circulation and metabolism
4. May assist in relieving stress-related headaches

Technique

Keep in mind that the eyes are delicate and pressure must be very light. Proper pressure points in the eye area are located inside the ocular bone. Pressure applied to the upper eyelid comes inside the bone just above the eyeball itself. When applying pressure to the lower lids, the fingers will actually be resting on the lashes and pressing on top of the lower ocular bone. Be sure to rest the back of the palms on the brow bone for added support. Both eyes will be done simultaneously so be careful to ensure even pressure on both sides.

1. Apply pressure with the middle or ring finger to the upper inner corner of eye just inside and under ocular bone.

2. Move to middle of upper eyelid; repeat pressure with same finger.

3. Move to outer corner of eye at junction of upper and lower eyelid; repeat pressure with same finger.

4. Apply pressure to temples with fingers or thumbs.

5. Repeat upper inner corner eyelid point.

6. Move to lower inner corner of eye at tear duct; apply lighter pressure with finger.

7. Move to lower middle lid; apply lighter pressure with same finger.

8. Move to outer corner of eye and apply similar pressure. (This point is the same location as for the outer corner of upper eyelid.)

9. Repeat temples.

SHIATSU FOR THE FULL BODY

There are some considerations to be kept in mind when doing *Shiatsu* on the body.

1. It's important to at least know main muscle groups and how to do effleurage, so a practical course in massage may be necessary.

2. *Shiatsu* for the body is similar in that the specific order may vary according to the need. If the full body is being done, the normal recommended order will be as follows: Front side of the body—foot, leg, other foot and leg, hand, arm, other hand and arm, head, chest, shoulders. Then the back side of the body—sole of foot, leg, other foot and leg, head, shoulders, upper arms, back.

3. In a full body treatment, about 35 minutes will be needed for the front side and 25 minutes for the back side.

4. Since there are many different sizes of bodies and hands, it's impossible to describe exactly how many points or rows are done

on the body. For simplicity, generally do three points each on smaller areas, eight points each on larger areas, and sixteen points along the spine.

5. For most areas, the thumbs will be used in an overlapping manner, but the four-finger vice-grip technique may also be used on some smaller areas such as the back of the upper arm.

6. As you move from one area of the body to another, be aware of the recipient's comfort level. The amount of pressure should be very light in certain areas such as the back of the knees and inner thighs. Pressure on the back may be much greater.

7. Always begin and end each area with effleurage.

8. Do not do *Shiatsu* on any areas of phlebitis or varicose veins, and be very cautious on a diabetic due to the predisposition to bruising.

FRONT SIDE

Purpose

1. *Shiatsu* relieves stress and tension in legs and arms.

2. Knees and ankles that are prone to water retention are relieved and the circulation is improved.

3. Circulation to the hands and feet is improved making the skin tone better, increasing nail growth, and providing an overall feeling of relaxation.

4. Stress and tension are relieved as the head, chest, and shoulders are done.

Technique

LEGS

1. Beginning with the foot of the left leg and starting with the little toe, pressure is applied with the thumb and first finger on the top and the sides between each joint of the toes. Keep pressure equal on both the thumb and finger. Work from the top/bottom of the tip of the toe inward to the base of the toe. The little toe and big toe normally have only two joints where the other toes have three. Do not apply pressure on the joints.

2. Moving from the toes to the top of the foot, pressure will be applied in four rows between the metatarsals and tarsals (bones of the foot to the ankle). Apply pressure to approximately three points between the base of the toe and the ankle in each row beginning at the outer side of the foot. Pressure is applied only to the top of the foot. See Figure 5-14. The soles of the feet will be done later when the recipient is lying on the stomach.

3. Ankles: This can be a step by itself or included with step two. Apply pressure in the center, and at the inside and outside of the ankle at the midpoint between the foot and calf where the ankle bends.

4. Using overlapped thumbs, apply pressure up the calf of the leg just outside the tibia (bone on front of calf). As you near the knee the angle of the line will veer to the outside where the final point is reached about three fingers below the knee and almost one inch to the outside. This last point is called the *Sanri* and is thought to be a central *Tsubo* for the general well-being of the entire body.

5. Apply pressure to three points below and above the knee.

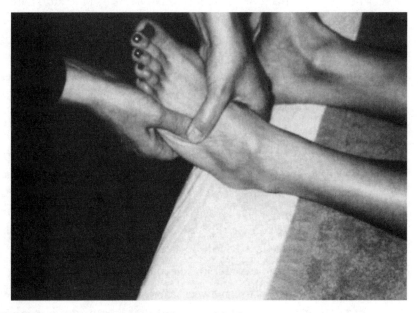

FIGURE 5-14 Apply pressure to the top of the foot.

6. The thigh is done in three rows; the top, then inside, then outside. Keep the leg straight to do the eight points up the center of the thigh (center of quadriceps). Then bend the leg out in order to use careful pressure up the inside of the thigh right in the middle. There is a very obvious dent between the muscles, and your hands should follow right along the dent to the base of the leg. Then straighten out the leg and apply pressure from the knee up the outer side of the leg and between the muscles to the base of the leg. Sometimes it's more convenient to face the leg from the side and apply thumb overlapping thumb pressure up the thigh.

7. Repeat steps one to six on the right leg.

ARMS

1. Moving to the fingers of the left hand, perform pressure between the joints of the top/bottom and sides of the fingers in a manner similar to that used with the toes. Start with the little finger and work in to the thumbs. Do not forget to do the thumbs. Use thumb and first fingers to do the fingers of the client.

2. The back and front of the hands are done next. First apply pressure on the metacarpals and carpals from the little finger to the first finger as was done for the feet. Four rows will be done with three points per row. The last row is the row from the base of the thumb to the wrist, so there are actually only three rows corresponding to the fingers themselves.

3. Turn to the inside of the hand, spread the fingers by inserting your little fingers between the thumb/first finger and the little finger/ring finger, and open the hand of the client. Apply pressure from the center of the base of the middle finger directly down the center of the hand (three points). Then follow around the padded part of the palm doing about six to eight points and ending at the fleshy part of the palm at the base of the thumb. Effleurage hands again and turn to the back of the hand.

4. Apply pressure to the center, inside, and outside of wrist.

5. Work up the lower arm between the extensor muscles from the wrist to slightly below the elbow and slightly outside. There is a

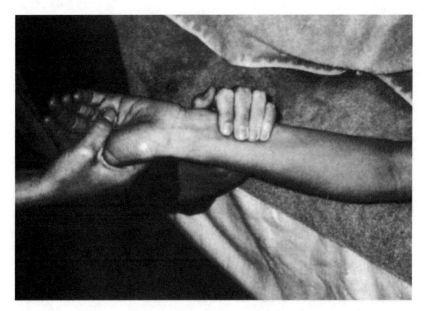

FIGURE 5-15 Begin to work up the arm, applying constant pressure.

Sanri point (the last point) on the lower arm similar to the same point on the calves of the legs. See Figure 5-15.

6. Apply pressure on the middle, inside, and outside of elbow. Turn to inside of lower arm.

7. Apply pressure in three rows up the inside lower arm, the middle, the inside, and the outside. Support the arm with your arm or place the arm on the bed to apply pressure.

8. Apply lighter pressure to the middle, inside, and outside of inner elbow.

9. Apply pressure in one row up the center of the upper arm. Turn to back of arm.

10. Apply pressure to outer arm while supporting the person's arm or putting it on the bed.

11. Repeat steps one to ten on the right hand and arm.

HEAD, NECK, CHEST

1. Move to the top of the head and apply pressure to the main head *Tsubo* on the crown with the pressure aiming toward the tip of the

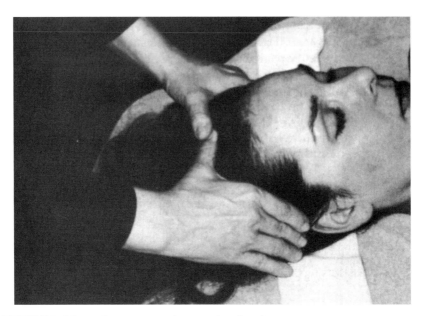

FIGURE 5-16 Apply pressure to the main head *Tsubo*.

feet. See Figure 5-16. Other head points may be done either by the full side hand vice-grip positioning or one at a time by the thumb overlap thumb technique. Do only the top of the head. The back of the head will be done when the person reverses position.

2. The face may be done as an option at this point. (Follow steps covered earlier in the chapter.) You may choose to just do a few strategic points, such as the forehead, temples, and inner corner of eyes.

3. The neck may be done (as outlined earlier) if desired or you may skip from the top of head to the chest.

4. The three rows of the chest are done as shown earlier in the chapter.

5. If desired, very light pressure may be done on the stomach/ abdominal area. Most often it is better to use the palms of the hands and apply pressure to four to six points in a clockwise direction around the navel, starting directly above the navel just below the rib cage (solar plexus area). See Figure 5-17.

After the final effleurage is done, remove any excess massage oil and apply powder to the entire body.

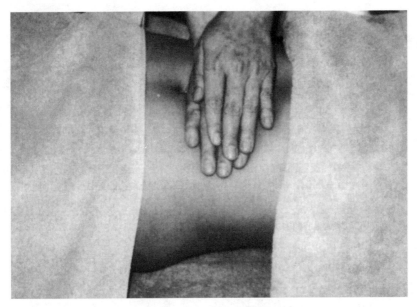

FIGURE 5-17 Using the palms, apply pressure around the navel.

BACK SIDE OF BODY

Purpose

1. The back side is normally the most relaxing part of any massage, and *Shiatsu* is no different. Although pressure to the back of the legs has to be lighter, greater pressure is exerted to the back for greater relaxation of the client.

2. *Shiatsu* on the back tremendously relieves stress and fatigue.

3. The knots and lumps in the shoulders from lactic acid buildup are relieved by *Shiatsu* of the back.

4. Keep in mind that all meridians start at the top of the head and end in the feet. Think of the meridians as paths going from the head to the feet. A good *Shiatsu* of the feet will work wonders for the circulation and well-being of the entire body. It can be equated to reflexology but without specific concentration on points for curative purposes.

Technique
LEGS

1. Starting at the bottom of the feet, you may do a very brief *Shiatsu* by applying pressure from the top of the foot in the center to the base of the foot in three points. However, for a full, deep-relaxing treatment, it is good to do more. If so, begin by applying pressure to the large pad of each toe.

2. Do pressure down the center row of the foot with deep-relaxing pressure (approximately three points).

3. As with the hands, apply pressure on about eight points working from the last midpoint on the heel around the foot and back to the same midpoint.

4. Apply pressure to the center of the ankle, then inside and outside.

5. Apply pressure from the ankle to the popliteal space behind the knee, concentrating the heavier pressure in the main body of the calf. There should be about eight points working up the center of the lower leg.

6. Apply much lighter pressure to the center, inside, and outside of the popliteal space. Be very careful in this area and avoid entirely if varicose veins exist or if it is too tender to the recipient.

7. The upper leg will be done in two rows, one row of about eight points up the center of the thigh and the second row on the outer thigh. Moving to the side and applying pressure in a thumb overlap thumb manner is effective for the outer thigh. See Figure 5-18.

HEAD/NECK

1. Apply pressure to the main crown point and then three points down the back of the head to the occipital. See Figure 5-19. If time allows, you may do three points in five rows as discussed earlier in the chapter. The main row and the base of the occipital are the most strategic points. Again, the base of the occipital should be done with the fingers in a deep lifting manner.

2. Apply pressure to the sides of the back of the neck with the thumb and four finger grip technique. See Figure 5-20.

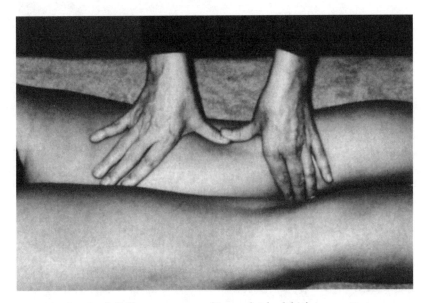

FIGURE 5-18 Apply lighter pressure working up back of thigh.

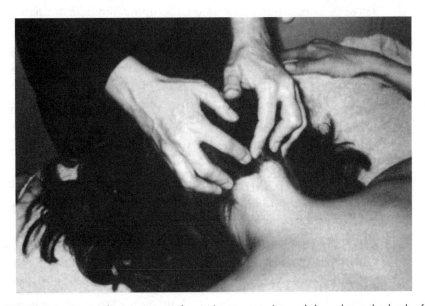

FIGURE 5-19 Apply pressure to the main crown point and then down the back of the head to the occipital.

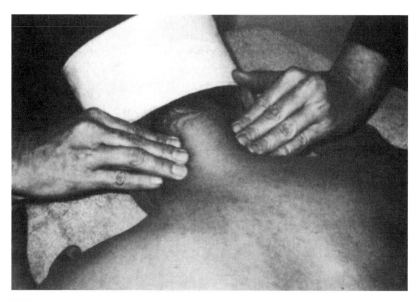

FIGURE 5-20 Apply pressure to the sides of the neck.

SHOULDERS/BACK

1. The top of the shoulders should be effleuraged again before and in between concentrated points on the upper shoulder (trapezius) area. A good five minutes should be spent on the shoulders, if necessary. The entire upper trapezius is prone to stress and fatigue, and you will find many tender areas that should be worked. However, do not apply pressure to the point of discomfort.

2. Apply pressure to approximately 16 points down the spine to the upper buttocks area. Pressure may be applied by both thumbs side by side on both sides of the spine at the same time if desired. See Figure 5-21. However, due to the potential for stress on the thumbs, you may choose to overlap the thumbs and work sideways down one side of the spine and then go around to the other side of the recipient to repeat the process down the other side.

3. Apply pressure with the base of the palms to the base of the back and upper buttock area. There will be one row of about three pressure points.

4. Moving back up to the scapula (shoulder blades) with a full back effleurage technique will position you well for the final *Shiatsu* area on the back. The *Tsubo* around the shoulder blades often

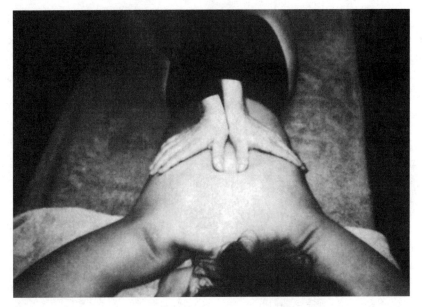

FIGURE 5-21 Work down the spine.

carry a lot of stress so apply pressure to about eight points following the anatomy of the shoulder blade from the top around to the base at the side of the recipient. Move to the other side and repeat on the other shoulder blade. If the *Tsubo* are difficult to locate, ask the person to put an arm behind the back to help you define the line by stroking the area. Then move the recipient's arm back to a comfortable position and apply pressure.

5. Even though the upper arms were done on the front side, it provides a very relaxing and comfortable ending to the *Shiatsu* to repeat the upper arm/top of outer shoulder points (approximately eight points) once more working from the top of the shoulder out to about the middle of the upper arm.

NOTE! *If you choose to do the buttocks, apply pressure across the top of the buttocks at the base of the back as done in step three. Then apply pressure around the coccyx bone in a clockwise manner. The final point will be a deep pressure from the side at the dimple in the buttocks with the thumb overlap thumb technique.*

To close the treatment, the final effleurage is done on the back, shoulders, and upper arms. Remove any massage oil and apply finishing body powder.

The recipient may be a little light-headed. Offer a glass of juice or water.

BACK TREATMENT

Purpose

1. A back *Shiatsu* massage can be a quick but very stress-relieving experience.
2. Everyone has stress and lactic acid buildup.
3. A back treatment takes very little time and can even be done in ten minutes, over clothes, anywhere.

Technique

1. Open with overall effleurage of the shoulders and back. Then apply pressure to the upper shoulders area in two or three rows of three points keeping close to the spinal column.
2. Apply pressure to approximately sixteen points down the spinal column as explained in the section for back on the full body.
3. Apply pressure with the base of the palms to the base of the back/upper buttocks. There will be one row of about three points.
4. Apply pressure around the scapula on each side of the spine locating points described in back section of full body.
5. Apply thumb four finger grip down the upper arms.
6. Finish with final full back effleurage. Remove any oil residue, and buff with body finishing powder. Cover back with towel, apply palm pressure down the sides of the spine and out the base of the back, and squeeze the upper arms.

HAND/ARM TREATMENT

Purpose

1. People carry more stress in hands and arms than is normally thought. *Shiatsu* in this area is very relaxing and stress relieving.

Technique

1. The technique will basically be the same as in a full body treatment, the main difference being that you will be sitting up and holding the client's hand/arm while working. *Shiatsu* for the hands will be done exactly as described in the full body treatment. Apply pressure on the fingers, back of hand, and inside of hand.

2. Apply pressure to the outside then the inside of the lower arm as shown in the full body treatment while supporting the arm with the other hand. Pressure will be done with one hand while the other hand supports the lower arm.

3. Apply pressure to the inside and outside three points of the elbow.

4. The upper arm is a little more difficult. You will hold the arm by the elbow with the forearm balanced over your arm. The other hand will apply pressure to the inner and outer sides of the upper arm. It may work well to use the thumb four finger grip if the arm is small enough.

5. Effleurage.

FOOT/LEG TREATMENT

Purpose

1. As has already been stated, the feet are the end points of the meridian system and a *Shiatsu* treatment for the feet alone will relieve stress and help the recipient relax.

Technique

1. The difference in the foot/leg treatment from the full body lies in the fact that you will be treating the recipient from a sitting position, and you will be seated in front of the recipient. The toes and top of the foot are done the same. After this is completed, lift the foot a little more and apply pressure to the points listed in the full body treatment on the sole of the foot only. Do not repeat the toes.

2. Apply pressure to the top, inside, outside of the ankles.

3. Apply pressure with a thumb over thumb technique up the calf. It is wise to hold the calf with both hands and gradually slide up to apply pressure. The back of the calf will be done with the fingers in the thumb four finger grip technique working from the bottom of the leg up to the knee.

4. Apply pressure to the three points below the knee.

5. Effleurage again.

CHAPTER
6

Reflexology

For centuries in the Orient, reflexology was the chosen source to evaluate the health of patients and the selected tool to create balance and harmony for the patient. If used properly, reflexology can offer relief for the minor discomforts of daily life. Headaches, backaches, stomach distress, indigestion, constipation, and menstrual cramps are just some of the problems that can be relieved through the manipulations of reflexology.

It is not a substitute for normal medical care; rather it is a holistic health support system.

THE TWO PHASES OF REFLEXOLOGY

Reflexology divides the body into ten zones, all vertical, from the left and right sides. Using the spine as the center point, each side has five zones. The right side of the zone represents the right side of the body and vice versa. For example, the first zone covers the area up and down the thumb and big toe. All the zones are worked on during both parts of the session.

Reflexology has two parts, the exploratory phase and the implementation phase. The more skilled you become in the first, the more successful you will be with the second. When you first start in reflexology, the exploratory phase will have great significance to the success of the implementation phase. Do not cut corners in taking exacting notes during the exploratory phase and refer to these notes when you begin the implementation phase.

The Exploratory Phase

The meridian points of the ears, hands, and feet reveal much about a person. With very slight pressure on any of these meridian points, a slight degree of pain might be felt. On some, actual pain may be involved and on other meridians, there will be no tenderness at all.

During the exploratory phase, you will go through the zones and seek out tiny crystallized deposits that surround the meridian point. The deposits feel like sand particles. Some will cluster together, giving the sensation of a group of wet sand granules rounded and bound up. The larger the cluster, the more tender the meridian point will be. Because it takes time for the cluster to develop, it means the nerve pathway has been affected for a longer period of time. It also represents the amount of time the body has been out of balance. Several reflexology sessions may be required to bring about an improvement.

CRYSTALS

The crystals you are searching for in the first phase are not magical rocks; they are deposits of calcium, uric acid, and other trace toxins in the blood. They accumulate when blood flow slows down. During the reduction of circulation, the calcium deposits create the surface crystals. When you break them apart, you increase the blood flow and increase the body's internal balancing program. Having the blood flow return to normal is a large part of obtaining the proper balance.

During a session, you will seek out a certain kind of tenderness that actually feels good even though it is overly sensitive. It will be a good "hurt." Apply firm but gently increasing pressure but be aware of the recipient's tolerance as meridian points are felt. Then back off the point, making sure that there is no pain or throbbing sensation once pressure stops. The pain in the meridian reflex lets you know that there is pain in the associated body part.

The meridian point is always round but the area of tenderness may take on a slightly different shape. However, it will always include the round reflex point. You have to locate the entire area that is tender to map out the area that doesn't hurt around the spot that does. Developing a proper evaluation sequence is important. Using the face of a clock as a guide to do the mapping-out process, mark the area that is tender and move clockwise away from the spot.

Careful evaluation and specific note-taking during the exploratory phase will enable you to provide an excellent implementation process. Do not underestimate the importance of the first part of the session. Do not rush through it. Without a strong foundation, the rest of your work will have poor results.

OTHER THEORIES

The medical community as a whole actually discounts the existence of crystals. They are not detected in any radiograph. Although physicians are trained to understand a great deal about anatomy, they are not trained to deal with the crystals.

Reflexologists strongly disagree with the medical community's concept. They are more holistic in nature and willingly accept the fact that they have not solved all the mysteries of the human body. They also accept that they can work with information without being able to fully explain its existence.

The Implementation Phase

The implementation phase or treatment session is the second part of reflexology. During this phase, detailed manipulations are performed to offer release of the recipient's problems. Once you have targeted the point, you begin to seek out the crystals. Your level of commitment, your ability to evaluate meridian points, and your handling of the crystals will determine your success.

Because the entire treatment is noninvasive, there are no side effects, which are frequent with many traditional medical treatments. Even without side effects, though, the actual implementation phase can be uncomfortable and sometimes truly painful. The skilled practitioner learns how to reduce the level of discomfort. Because everyone's pain threshold or tolerance is different, it is important to assess the sensitivity of the recipient.

You must become familiar with the various meridian points found on any ear, hand, or foot. These special points have direct links with the organs and the skeletal system. This is the hardest and most challenging aspect of understanding reflexology. The better you are at evaluating the ear, hand, and foot, the better you will be at executing the implementation phase.

When one meridian point is triggered, others around it will sense the trigger and slowly activate also. Because an entire section can be activated by one triggering contact, reflexology can rebalance the entire body.

When you work on someone, you must learn which meridian points are closely interconnected. It is advisable to work connecting points all at the same time, which will gain a better result than working just one single meridian point. Following are some of the interconnecting meridian points.

- The digestive system includes the kidneys, liver, pancreas, stomach, intestines, bladder, and colon (ascending, descending, and transverse).

- The reproduction system includes the ovaries, uterus, and Fallopian tubes in women, so you would do all the meridian points on the woman's foot or hand.

- The endocrine system includes the pituitary, thyroid, adrenal, and thymus glands.

Reflexology will be able to ease most discomforts from conditions such as tension headaches, mild sinus congestion, menstrual cramps, and constipation. These conditions are not life-threatening and the body handles them with or without assistance.

A person experiencing headaches caused by eyesight troubles, mild concussions, sinus infections, or cramping caused by miscarriage should see a physician.

SPECIFIC AREAS OF CONCENTRATION

The "magic" of reflexology is its ability to cover so many parts of the body from the soft organs to the skeletal system. Because you are not medically trained, only the conditions typical of everyday stresses and strains are included.

The joy of reflexology lies in its ability to aid so many different conditions. Although it is not common for a single session to bring complete relief from most problems, it will start the process. Following are specific ailments that plague the average person. These conditions were chosen because they do not cross into the medical or disease arena.

Headaches

This condition is especially common. One of the best reasons to choose reflexology over taking aspirin or other medication is that the drugs circulate in the entire bloodstream, which means they are medicating the whole body for relief of only the headache. In the case of aspirin and all the extra-strength versions, the stomach lining is directly attacked.

You can choose meridian points on the ears, hands, or feet to offer relief.

ON THE EAR

There are two points at the top of the outer ear. One point is for the headache that is felt in front of the forehead and eye area. The second point is for the headache that seems to send pain to the back of the head. See Figure 6-1.

Determine if the headache is felt more on the left side, perhaps behind the left eye or at the left temple. That would direct your treatment to begin on the left ear. The points are at the exact same spot on either ear. Place your thumb pad on the top, front side of the ear, where the curve of the ear begins to curl. Next, place your first finger pad on the back side of the exact point. Press gently but firmly on the point and hold for the count of three. Release your pressure and, following a clockwise circular pattern,

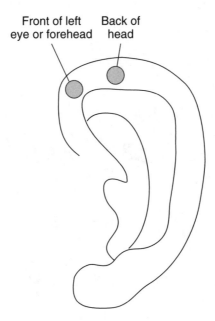

Front of left eye or forehead   Back of head

FIGURE 6-1 Pressure points on the left ear for treating headaches. Points are the same for both ears.

massage that point to the count of four. Stop, replace the firm pressure on the point, and hold for the count of three. Then begin the massage movement in a counter-clockwise pattern to the count of four. Repeat these steps twice. Release the ear from your fingers. There should be a reduction in the headache pain. It should take between five and ten minutes for the sensation to go away completely. It is advisable to work both ears. Repeat the exact same procedure on the meridian points on the right ear.

You can repeat this procedure several times. If the person has a history of chronic headaches, you will need to work on him or her three times a day for five days. This may seem like a lot of time, but you are readjusting the pattern of the pressure that has been building up in the person's head for a long time. The results are always worth it in the end.

ON THE HAND

Determine if the headache is felt more on the left side, perhaps behind the left eye or at the left temple. That would direct your treatment to begin on the left hand. The points are at the exact same spot on either hand. Each fingertip is part of the meridian point that reflects the head. See Figure 6-2.

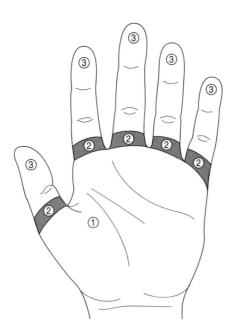

FIGURE 6-2 Pressure points on the left hand for treating headaches. 1, web; 2, left eye/left sinus; 3, head. For right hand, use right eye/right sinus.

The base of each finger reflects the eyes and sinuses. Even the fleshy part of the thumb pad reflects the head as do the tops of the fingers. The base of the fingers represent the lower sections of the neck and throat. One point that is not easily explained is the center of the web tissue between the thumb and the index finger. It is a wonderful point to release intensive headaches caused by stress. The confusion comes with the soft tissue that connects the thumb and the index finger. There is a strong nerve cell that lies in the center of this web tissue that can release the pressures of a normal headache. Ancient writings referred to this area as the "third eye."

Place your thumb on the top of the web tissue and your index finger on the palm side to complete the cycle. Press your thumb toward your index finger, trying to get them to touch, which, of course, is not possible. The pressure you use is strong. Hold the point to the count of five, releasing the intense pressure, but not moving off the point. Repeat this technique three or four times.

ON THE FOOT

The top of the big toe on each foot reflects the head, and the base of each toe reflects the eyes and sinuses. See Figure 6-3. The left foot affects the

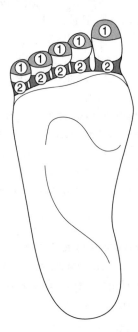

FIGURE 6-3 Pressure points on the foot for treating headaches. 1, left side of the head; 2, left eye/left sinus. For right foot, use right side of head, right eye/right sinus.

left side of the body and vice versa. Determine which side of the body has the pain sensation and begin your treatment on that side.

Pressing firmly and pumping gently, use the opposite hand's index finger for support of the toe when you apply direct pressure on the zone point. Repeat the pressing pumping action three times on each toe. Then move onto the base of each toe. Instead of finding a meridian point and applying direct pressure, roll the base of the toes between your thumb pad and your index finger. Make small pressurized circles over each individual toe. Do all the toes on each foot.

Then use your thumb pad again and press on each meridian on the top of each toe that corresponds to the head. Finally, place your thumb on the center of the fleshy part of the big toe and press very firmly for a count of five. Release the pressure, but do not move off the meridian. Repeat the pressure hold three times.

Backaches

More people are seated in front of computer terminals than ever before. This creates pressure in the spinal cord, particularly in their upper back, shoulder, and neck area. Whether a corporate executive or a college student, people find themselves forcing pressure against their vertebrae. In addition, heavy schedules during the work week force people to cram too much into their weekends. They can have a schedule of cleaning, washing the car, watching their children play sports, shopping, gardening, and socializing in the evening. Their backs are sure to take a direct hit from these events.

In addition, more people are buying at-home fitness workout equipment, and many of them are experiencing backaches and strains after using these machines and apparatus without the professional assistance they would find in a gym or exercise club. The following discussion pertains to people with mild backache and back soreness.

*It is **not** recommended that you attempt to use reflexology on someone who is experiencing back pain due to an accident or specific trauma, or a disease such as spinal meningitis.*

ON THE EAR

The outer edges of the ears reflect the spinal column. For this condition, you can determine which ear to manipulate by finding out which is the person's dominant side. Begin your treatment with the left ear for a right-handed person and vice versa. See Figure 6-4.

Roll the outer edge of the ear between your thumb and your first finger, starting at the base of the earlobe and working upward to the top of the ear. Your finger pressure should be firm and your movements smooth, similar to a regular massage movement. Then reverse your direction. It is a good practice to work all the meridian points reflecting the spinal column; therefore, repeat this procedure twice on each ear.

ON THE HAND

The outer edge of both thumbs along with the base of each hand reflect the entire skeletal column from the top of the neck to the base of the spine through the area called the tail bone or coccyx. Work on the non-dominant hand first. Using your thumb, manipulate the meridian points

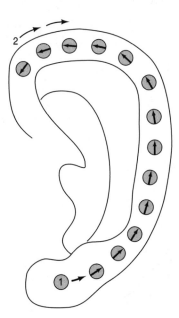

FIGURE 6-4 Pressure points on the ear for treating backaches. Step one moves up the ear; step two moves down the ear.

on the thumb and base of the hand depending on where the soreness is on the person's back. Upper backache is on the upper part of the outer edge of the thumb. Lower back pain is reflected on the lower edge of the thumb and the base of the hand. See Figure 6-5.

Use very firm pressure, working slowly over the designated area. Each point is pressed independently. Your thumb moves along the edge of the thumb, as if there were vertebrae one after the other along the edge. Repeat the firm, slow pressure four times. Work down the thumb and base and then reverse direction and work upward. Manipulate meridians on both hands.

ON THE FOOT

Similar to the outer edge of the thumbs, the entire skeletal column is reflected along the outer edges of the big toe and along the instep and

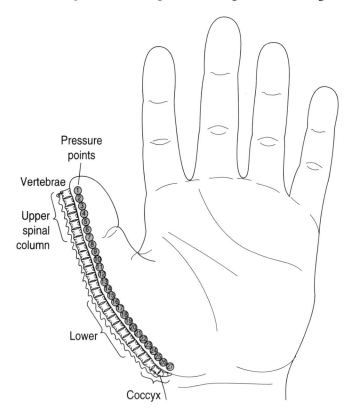

FIGURE 6-5 Pressure points on the palm for treating backaches. Points are the same for the right hand.

heel. The meridian points are the same on the left and right foot. See Figure 6-6.

Manipulate the right foot for a left-handed person and vice versa. Determine where the pain is located—upper, middle, or lower back. The meridian points begin for the head and neck on the big toe's outer edge; the middle of the back is in the instep and the lower back follows along the top of the heel. The coccyx is at the base of the heel.

Use your thumb pad and manipulate each meridian independently. Work your thumb downward, using slow, firm pressure. Then reverse direction. Repeat this pressure motion five times.

Digestion Troubles

In today's society, people are rushed throughout the day and making time to relax and eat slowly is often difficult. Fast food is making it impossible to think about slowing down the time it takes to eat. Eating hurriedly forces the stomach to digest partially chewed food in an atmosphere of time constraints and physical and emotional stress. In addition to bad eating habits,

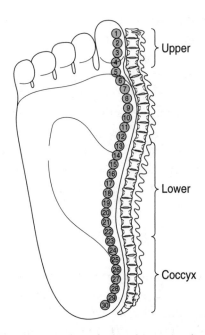

FIGURE 6-6 Pressure points on the right foot for treating backaches. Points are the same for the left foot.

our metabolism slows down and becomes less efficient as we age. The end result of all of these factors is an increase in heartburn and stomachaches.

Reflexology can assist in two areas. First is the relief of minor stomachaches caused by simple daily stress or bad eating habits. The treatment technique described in the following paragraphs addresses those situations. Another benefit of reflexology is the tracking of an **ulcer.** There will be crystal clusters in the meridian points relating to the stomach when an ulcer is developing. Even when you destroy the clusters, however the person will need medical attention.

> *Ulcers are a serious medical problem that should not be ignored. The two most common kinds of ulcers are the peptic ulcer and the duodenal ulcer in the upper portion of the small intestine. The duodendum lies right next to the stomach. The powerful stomach acids seep into the lining of the duodendum, causing the ulcers to form.*

A physician should always be consulted regarding any stomach ailments. With the doctor's approval, reflexology can be used as part of the treatment to reduce discomfort.

The reflexology exploratory phase can alert people that trouble is developing and direct them in the proper medical direction. In this situation, reflexology becomes an effective preventive treatment so an ulcer does not progress to the point of requiring surgery.

Other stomachaches are created from the previously mentioned lifestyle choices. Although they are not serious, that does not diminish the discomfort surrounding them. Here, reflexology can provide immediate release of the discomfort.

ON THE HAND

The stomach's meridian points are on the left hand in the center of the palm. See Figure 6-7. There is no single spot the size of a dot to look for, but as you begin learning how to work with reflexology, you will get accustomed to finding this area. Using your dominate hand's thumb, locate the center of the meridian point area.

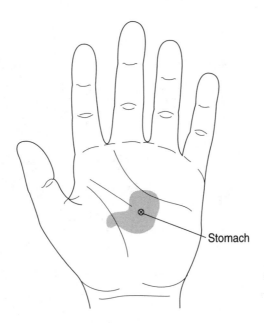

FIGURE 6-7 Pressure point area on the palm for treating digestion problems. Points are the same for the right palm.

Begin by moving in small circles in a counter-clockwise motion over the center area of the meridian points. Make three small circles. Stop and place direct pressure on the center meridian with your thumb pad. Repeat the small circles for three rotations in a clockwise pattern.

ON THE FOOT

The stomach's meridian points are on the left foot on the outside section of the instep. Just as on the hand, there is not a single dot to look for. See Figure 6-8 for help in locating it. Using your dominant hand's thumb, locate the center of the meridian point area. Begin by moving in small circles in a counter-clockwise motion over the center area of the meridian points. Make three small circles. Stop and place direct pressure on the center meridian with your thumb pad. Then repeat the small circles for three rotations in a clockwise pattern. The foot is much stronger in getting reflexology to respond to the inner body. It is possible to bring relief quickly to a person with stomach cramps.

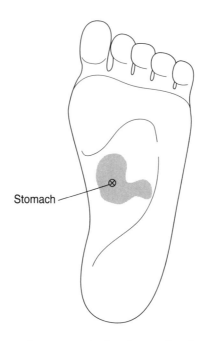

Stomach

FIGURE 6-8 Pressure point area on the foot for treating digestion problems. Points are the same for the right foot.

Pregnancy

This is the most important event in a woman's life. It is filled with wonderment and worry. For the first-time pregnant woman the experience is filled with questions, some of which have difficult answers. But the query "Can reflexology help make it an easier pregnancy?" is an easy one to answer—yes, absolutely, positively yes! Reflexology will make an easy pregnancy even more comfortable and a difficult pregnancy less traumatic. However, reflexology cannot make a difficult pregnancy easy.

With the woman's body going through so many changes, the meridian points/reflexes are put on high alert. Everything on and in the body is more noticeable.

Special indigestion problems can occur during pregnancy. Morning sickness can make eating an unpleasant experience. As the baby grows and the body expands, the baby increases pressure on the stomach, intestines, and **diaphragm.** The expectant mother can struggle with stomach problems for several months, during which time she cannot take medications. In addition, a pregnant woman's feet will often swell and bloat. She frequently feels she needs extra attention, and her mood swings can be particularly strong.

Selecting reflexology as a source of relief is the perfect answer. Mild depression, swollen hands and feet, constipation, intestinal distress, headaches, backaches, and nausea can all be aided, and it is perfectly safe for the baby.

During the nine months, certain ailments and conditions will become more prevalent. Use reflexology to alleviate whatever discomfort is bothering the woman at the time. For example, through the first trimester, morning sickness may dominate, and through the last trimester she may have more problems with her bladder and bowels.

You can combine several reflexology treatments, all of which can be done while the pregnant woman is in a moderately reclining position. Do not have her lie flat on her back.

Premenstrual Syndrome

Premenstrual syndrome (PMS) was misunderstood by doctors and the general public for centuries. Not all women experience PMS, but those who do are familiar with the pain, emotional swings, and overall reduction of self-esteem that occurs during the time between ovulation and the actual blood flow of their menses.

Certain patterns now help us determine when the PMS attacks will occur. Hormone surges are a major cause of the problem. Women will often complain of tenderness in their breasts, and headaches are often a side effect. Reducing the intake of caffeine and salt often helps.

ON THE HAND

To reduce stress associated with PMS, you will need to work all the points for the entire reproduction system, including the meridians for the **solar plexus, adrenal gland, pituitary gland,** and the brain. See Figure 6-9. The solar plexus is on both hands, at the center of the palm. The adrenal gland point is on both hands, at the fleshy part below the thumb. The point for the pituitary gland and brain is the same and is on the fleshy part of the thumb.

Use your dominant thumb and use pressing and pumping motions on all of these points. Do the complete rotations four times. Work the ovary points, then the uterus and Fallopian tube meridian points, followed by

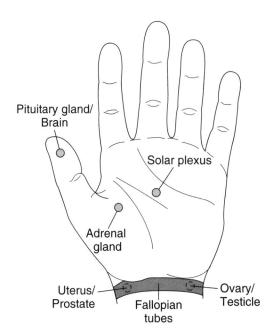

FIGURE 6-9 Pressure points on the palm for treating stress associated with premenstrual syndrome. Points are the same for the right hand.

the solar plexus and adrenal gland, and finally the pituitary and brain points.

ON THE FOOT

The same points on the hands will be duplicated on the feet, and they are even more responsive there. The solar plexus is on both feet at the lower edge of the balls of the feet. The adrenal gland is on both feet at the top section of the instep, on the inside edge. The point for the pituitary gland and brain is the same and is on both feet on the fleshy part of the big toes. See Figure 6-10.

Use your dominant thumb and use pressing and pumping motions on all of these points. Do the complete rotations four times. Work the ovary points, then the uterus and Fallopian tube meridian points, followed by the solar plexus and adrenal gland, and finally the pituitary and brain points.

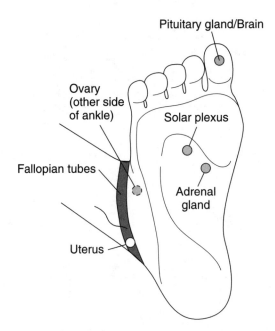

Pituitary gland/Brain

Ovary
(other side
of ankle)

Solar plexus

Fallopian tubes

Adrenal
gland

Uterus

FIGURE 6-10 Pressure points on the foot for treating stress associated with premenstrual syndrome. Points are the same for the left foot.

Menstrual Cramps

ON THE HAND

The left hand reflects the left ovary and vice versa. Once you determine which ovary is causing the cramps, you work that meridian point. See Figure 6-11. Place your dominant thumb on the outside edge of the base of the wrist. Apply gentle but firm pressure on the meridian, and then pump the point four times. Move your thumb on the other side of the base of the wrist and repeat the same procedure.

Then place your index finger along the top side of the wrist, as you slide your thumb along the base of the inside of the wrist. Slide your thumb back and forth three times. This is the meridian point for the Fallopian tube. It is not necessary to do both ovaries and Fallopian tubes, but it would not be damaging to do all the meridian points either. Working these meridians 48 hours before ovulation begins will help lessen the chance that any cramping will occur. The same is true for the 48-hour time frame before the menses begins.

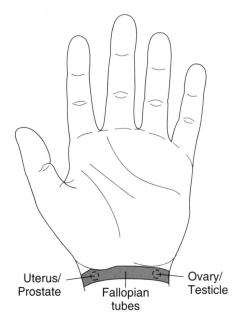

Uterus/   Ovary/
Prostate   Testicle
                  Fallopian
                    tubes

FIGURE 6-11 Pressure points on the palm for treating menstrual cramps. Points are the same on right hand.

ON THE FOOT

This precautionary treatment is also effective on the feet. The left foot reflects the left side of the reproduction system and vice versa. The meridian for the uterus is on the right foot. Ask which side is cramping. See Figure 6-12.

Place your dominant thumb on the outside space below the ankle of the corresponding side. Your index finger is on the inside space. Apply gentle but firm pressure on the meridian and then pump the point four times. Move your thumb on the top side of the area where the foot meets the leg and slide your thumb along this area. Slide your thumb back and forth three times. Gentle pressing and pumping are also required. It is not necessary to do both sides, but it cannot hurt the system if you do.

Sinus Problems

Many factors can create sinus inflammation. Heredity is one; if the parents have conditions that cause stress on the sinus sacs, they can pass on the tendency to their children. Allergies can be hereditary or just a weakness in one's own immune system. Bacteria and viruses can also irritate

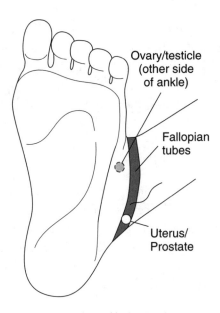

FIGURE 6-12 Pressure points on the ankle for treating menstrual cramps. Points are the same on right ankle.

the sacs. Often the eyes, nose, and temples will be sensitive when the sinus sacs are inflamed. There are six sacs—two under the eyebrows, two at the temples, and two under the eye sockets.

Medications have strong side effects. Pills can cause drowsiness, and nasal sprays can be addictive. The body can build up a resistance to many medications. This forces the person to either increase the dosage or find stronger formulas to get the sinuses back to normal. Unfortunately, with the constant use of medications, the sinuses seldom return to normal. The medications will leave a trace of drug within the sinus cavity after the person stops taking it. A dependency slowly builds inside the sinus sac, causing the person to continue using the medications for longer periods of time. Reflexology can help relieve the pressure and aid the body's ability to drain the sinuses with zero side effects.

ON THE HAND

To relieve the sinuses, it is important to manipulate other connected areas (eyes, throat, neck, and head). The meridian points for the sinuses and the eyes are the same zones. The base of each finger on the left hand reflects the sinus and eye on the left side of the body; the right hand works for the right side. See Figure 6-13. On either hand, the bottom of the first digit and the base of the thumb have reflective meridians for the head, neck, and throat. Place your thumb on the meridian point, apply firm pressure, and hold for the count of five. Then pump the zone for the count of three. Work each finger and thumb separately. Repeat this procedure three times.

ON THE FOOT

The eyes and sinus points are on the base of each toe. The left foot reflects the left side of the body and vice versa. The throat and neck are at the base of the big toes. See Figure 6-14. Use your thumb on each meridian point individually. Place your thumb on the meridian point, apply firm pressure, and hold for the count of five. Then pump the zone for the count of three. Work each finger and thumb separately. Repeat this procedure three times.

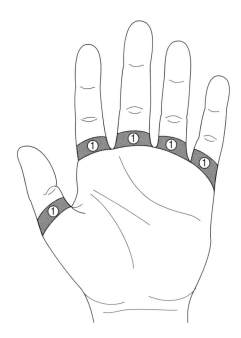

FIGURE 6-13 Pressure points on the palm for treating sinus problems. 1, sinus drains. Points are the same on right hand.

Overall Balance

Sometimes a person does not have any one body area that is causing a problem, but just feels out of sorts for no known reason. The classic "umbrella" rationale for this is stress.

We recognize that there is good stress along with negative stress. When people complain that they are just not feeling like themselves, or that their sleep patterns are broken, they are looking for answers. Reflexology can bring balance back to their bodies. Working all the meridian points in either their hands or feet will accomplish this task.

You can also use this treatment routine along with others for a complete wellness program. Depression, pregnancy, stress reduction, and indigestion are just some of the many conditions that would benefit by adding this routine to the manipulations for the specific conditions.

This is one of the most universal treatments available. It will blend with all of the other treatment segments or stand on its own merit.

ON THE EAR

Start at the very top of the outer edge of the ear, working all the way down to the earlobe. Use your thumbs and index fingers of both hands, and work both of the person's ears at the same time. Place your thumb on the inside of the rim and the index finger behind to support the pressure of the thumb. Slowly and firmly work all the meridian points, from the top of the ear to the end of the earlobe. Put pressure on each reflex point and hold the pressure to the count of four. Move to the next point. Repeat this gentle firm pressure cycle over the entire ear. See Figure 6-15 for the location of each meridian point.

When you have completed the movement, stop and place your fingers over the ears to gently caress the entire ear for a holding pattern of three seconds. Lift your hands off the ears. Ask if the person feels more relaxed. If the answer is no, repeat the entire process.

ON THE HAND

Start with the top of the body, by beginning with the fingertips on the person's nondominant hand. Using your thumb, manipulate the top portion of the person's thumb, which is the reflex point for the brain, with a pumping action. Work the meridian three times. Then proceed to pump

FIGURE 6-14 Pressure points on the foot for treating sinus problems. 1, sinus drains. Points are the same on right foot.

the tops of each finger separately. You are working the reflex points for the brain on each finger. Gentle but firm pressure should be used.

Next work the reflex points for the spinal column that run along the outer edge of the thumb, down along the base toward the wrist. See Figure 6-16. These are the meridian points for the entire spinal column, a major center in which stress can build when the body's inner balance is off. Move your thumb along the meridians by sliding down the outer edge of the person's thumb, very slowly. Then use tiny circles to work in an upward direction. Repeat the sliding down and circling back upward three or four times.

Repeat the entire process on the dominant hand. Ask if the person feels more at ease. If needed, repeat the entire process on both hands two or three times. Give the person's body at least 10 to 12 minutes to respond. Reflexology is effective, but it does take time to get the relay to the brain and back again.

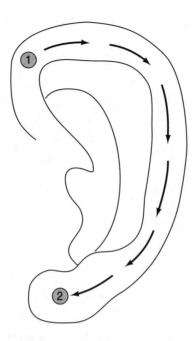

FIGURE 6-15 Pressure points on the ear for treating overall balance. 1, beginning point; 2, ending point.

ON THE FOOT

The reflexes on the feet are the most powerful for regaining inner balance. The meridian points for the head are on the tops of the toes. At the middle of the big toe is the reflective point of the brain. The spinal column responds to the outer edge of the big toe to the instep and down to the edge of the heel. See Figure 6-17.

Pump the meridian on the top of the big toe three or four times. Then pump the tops of each toe separately, twice. You are working the reflex point for the brain that is on each toe. Gentle but firm pressure should be used.

Next work the reflex points for the spinal column. They run along the outer edge of the big toe, along the base and down the inner edge of the foot to the base of the heel. These are the meridian points for the entire spinal column. Move your thumb along the meridians by very slowly slid-

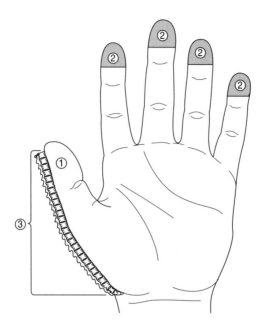

FIGURE 6-16 Pressure points on the palm for treating overall balance. 1, brain reflex; 2, brain reflex; 3, spinal reflex.

ing down the outer edge of the client's big toe, continuing down the inside edge to the heel. Then use tiny circles to work in an upward direction. Repeat the sliding down and circling back upward twice.

Repeat the entire process on the other foot. Ask if the person feels more at ease. If needed, repeat the entire process on both feet, two or three times. Give the client's body at least 10 to 12 minutes to respond. Remember that it takes time to get the relay to the brain and back again.

Depression

People who have serious or long-standing problems with depression need to seek medical assistance. The reasons for a person to feel depressed can be complex. Just handling the daily events of our lives will occasionally make us feel negative, and we cannot expect every day to be a joy and to feel all at peace with the world. Even listening to a news broadcast can make us feel uneasy, so it is not surprising that we can feel depressed several times a day.

Many factors can cause people to become depressed. Some people try to assume their entire family's problems, believing it is their job to solve everyone's dilemmas. These people are setting themselves up for discord

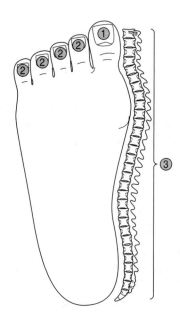

FIGURE 6-17 Pressure points on the top of the foot for treating overall balance. 1, brain reflex; 2, brain reflex; 3, spinal reflex.

and stress. The trend in America is toward more single-parent households. Those parents are forced to take on much more responsibility than they originally expected when they decided to become a family. Single parents are great candidates for stress reduction. If they do not find a way to vent the pressures of everyday problems, they will develop signs of depression. Left unhandled, they can become fully depressed and begin a negative spiral downturn, making it impossible to run their household efficiently.

Depression can also come from dealing with anger. Some people hold in their anger to the point that it begins to eat at them from the inside. Besides developing ulcers and blazing headaches, the anger causes the brain to shut down and depression begins.

These situations require professional assistance. Reflexology can help reduce certain stress levels and offer a tranquil place for true relaxation. However, it will not solve the underlying problems.

Begin with soft music and lower the lights to create a calming atmosphere. Make sure that you change your voice to a very soft-spoken tone. By slowing down your speech, you will automatically create a more peaceful speaking voice. Most people speed up their speech when they are edgy, out of sorts, or feeling pressure.

The reflexology session will concentrate on the nervous system. The key glands are the adrenal, pituitary, and **pineal.** The diaphragm helps regulate a steadier breathing pattern and the voice. The brain needs some special TLC; because you cannot offer it any other way, reflexology is the best way to make it feel at peace. You will work on all the meridian points for each of these glands, the diaphragm, and the brain. It is advisable to work the ears, hands, and feet. If you want to work only one area, then do the feet.

ON THE EAR

The main reflex point is for the brain, which is at the top of the outer ridge of the ear. See Figure 6-18. Work both ears at the same time. Place your thumb pad on the inside of the meridian point. Back the thumb with the support of your index finger by placing it behind the ear. Hold the reflex point to the count of five and release.

ON THE HAND

You need to work on the reflex points for the pituitary, pineal, and adrenal glands; the diaphragm; and the brain. Both hands will be manipulated.

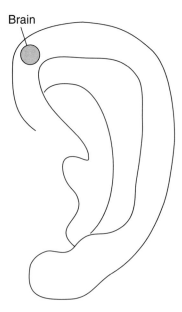

FIGURE 6-18 Pressure point on the ear for treating depression

The meridian point for the brain is at the top part of the thumb pad. The meridian for the pituitary and pineal glands is the same point, in the center of the pad area. The diaphragm's meridian runs across the entire palm on both hands. The reflex point for adrenal glands is at the top part of the fleshy area beneath the base of the thumb on both hands. See Figure 6-19.

Start by working on the client's nondominant hand, beginning with the reflex for the brain. Place your thumb over it and apply a firm pumping action for three or four seconds. Then slide down to the meridian point for the pituitary and pineal glands. Pump this point with your thumb for four seconds. Make five counter-clockwise circles over this point, pump again for three seconds, and reverse the movement to clockwise.

Slide your thumb down to the reflex for the adrenal gland, pump for three seconds, and follow with five counter-clockwise circles. Pump again for three seconds, and reverse the movement to clockwise.

Lastly, slide your thumb to the center of the palm and pump the meridian ribbon in the center point for two to three seconds. Then slide your thumb over the entire meridian ribbon from the inner to the outer edge five or six times, making small clockwise circles while you work from side to side.

Repeat the process on the dominant hand.

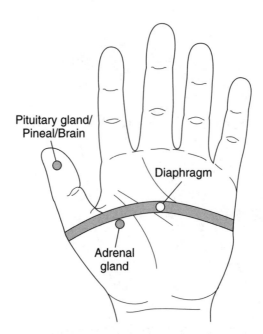

FIGURE 6-19 Pressure points on the palm from treating depression

ON THE FOOT

You will work on both feet, but start on the client's nondominant side. The brain reflex point is on the top of the big toe on both feet. Pump this meridian three times.

Slide down a short distance to the center of the fleshy part of the big toe, which is where the meridian point for the pituitary and pineal glands lies. Pump this point four times.

The diaphragm is at the very top of the arch or, for flat-footed people, it is at the bottom of the ball of the foot. Glide your thumb to the area at the top of the arch. This is where the diaphragm meridian ribbon lies. It is not a singular point but flows from one side of the foot to the other. See Figure 6-20. Place your thumb in its center point and pump it for three seconds. Then work across the entire meridian ribbon by moving in counter-clockwise circles in one direction, and clockwise circles in the other.

The adrenal gland's meridian point is close to the diaphragm. Dividing the width of the foot in half, on the right foot it is slightly to the right of center; on the left foot it is close to the center. Figure 6-20 will help you

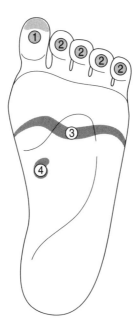

FIGURE 6-20 Pressure points on the foot for treating depression. 1, pituitary/pineal/brain; 2, brain; 3, diaphragm; 4, adrenal gland.

find these meridians. Once you have located the meridian, pump it with your thumb with firm pressure for five or six seconds.

Constipation

Nearly everyone has had the sensation of not being able to move the bowels, called constipation. Some of the more common causes are

- Various eating habits, such as eating very late at night.
- Poor eating habits, including insufficient roughage or fiber in the diet.
- Eating too quickly so that food is only partly chewed.
- Lifestyle factors such as a high-stress job.

Occasional irregularity is not usually a problem. The body's internal system will work it all out. However, for the person with a constant or daily bout of constipation, a problem exists. First, the person should see an internist to ensure that a serious medical problem such as a blocked intestine, twisted colon, or early stages of colitis is not the cause of the constipation.

Constipation can be a side effect of many medications. Only a doctor can decide if the need for drugs outweighs the side effects. Illness can also cause constipation, forcing bacteria counts to grow too high. This is another reason it is imperative to seek medical attention if the constipation is not just a short-term, nonregular condition.

ON THE HAND

The hands and feet are the areas to work on. The feet are the first choice because the meridians on the feet are more reactive than those on the hands. On the hands the meridians are located as follows: the descending colon is on the left, next to the meridian for the intestines. The meridian for the descending colon is close to the inner edge of the palm, underneath the thumb. The large and small intestines are under the stomach reflex point. They encompass the lower third of the palm area. The anus is at the bottom edge of the palm, right before the wrist area. It is the same on both hands. The meridian for the ascending colon is on the right hand on the outer edge of the palm, underneath the pinky finger. The reflex for the intestines is in the middle of the lower one-third of the palm area. The ileocecal valve is on the right hand only; it has a singular meridian point that is located on the outer edge of the hand. See Figure 6-21 for the exact location.

You might want to work with the nondominant hand first, but because the reflex areas are found on both, you can begin on either hand. You should notice that there is not just a singular point, but rather a large area for the intestines and colon sections. Find the areas, as described above.

Start with the ascending colon reflex. Place your thumb pad over it as much as possible. Press very firmly, and hold the pressure to the count of ten. Release and begin tiny clockwise circles over the area. Continue working the circles for three to four seconds. Then slide down to the intestinal reflex area and apply firm pressure over it for ten seconds. Release and begin tiny clockwise circles over the area. Continue working the circles for three seconds.

Slide over to the descending colon. Apply firm pressure over it for ten seconds. Release and begin tiny clockwise circles over the area. Continue working the circles for three seconds. Locate the anus meridian as described above. Place your thumb pad on it and pump the point for five to seven seconds.

If you are working on the right hand, locate the reflex for the ileocecal valve. Place your thumb pad on the reflex and pump the point to the

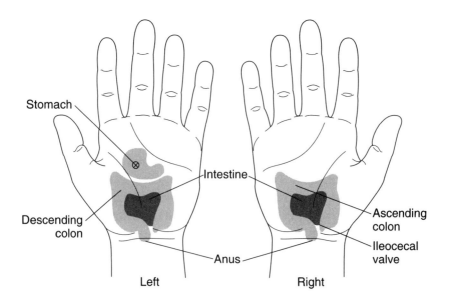

FIGURE 6-21 Pressure points on the hands for treating constipation

count of four. Stop and place constant pressure on the reflex for three seconds. Repeat this two-step process twice. Switch to begin working on the other hand. If you had been working on the left hand, do the ileocecal meridian now.

Next work with the reflective area for the intestines, as described above. Apply firm pressure over it for ten seconds. Release and begin tiny clockwise circles over the area. Continue working the circles for three seconds. Slide over to the decending colon reflective area. Place your thumb pad over it as much as possible. Press very firmly, and hold the pressure to the count of ten. Release and begin tiny clockwise circles over the area. Continue working the circles for three to four seconds.

It should take about half an hour to take effect. Have the person relax and stay near a bathroom. The first reaction he or she will experience is the gas that has accumulated in the intestinal tract and colon. The fecal material will continue to process the gas even though it won't release out of the body. People occasionally release the gas during the treatment and become embarrassed. It is very important to make them understand that this is what their bodies need to do.

It is a good idea to have an oscillation fan turned on before beginning. The air will move throughout the session and will minimize the discomfort of the client. Flatulence may not occur this quickly, but it will occur before the release is complete. Tell the person what is to happen so that he or she can be properly prepared.

ON THE FOOT

The feet are the stronger resource to get the release to occur. The same number of meridian points are engaged and, as with the hands, you work both feet. See Figure 6-22.

Because the right foot has the ileocecal valve meridian point, it would be good to start with the right foot. Begin with the transverse colon reflex located in the center of the arch. It is not a singular point, so place your thumb over the area and press firmly for three seconds. Release the pressure and switch to a pumping movement for the count of three. Slide over to the meridian point for the ascending colon. Do the exact same movements you just completed on the transverse colon reflex point.

The small intestine meridian area is beside the ascending colon, but slightly to the right. Place your thumb over the area and pump it for five to six seconds. Then move to the singular meridian point for the ileocecal

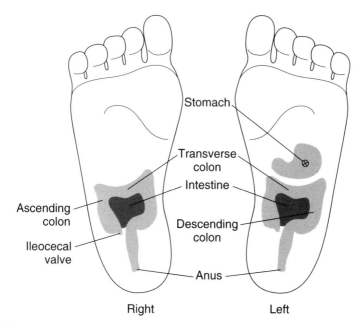

FIGURE 6-22 Pressure points on the feet for treating constipation

valve. Apply firm pressure with your thumb pad on the point. Hold to the count of six. Move down to the meridian point for the anus, located at the center of the base of the heel. Apply firm pressure to the count of three. Release the pressure and make small clockwise movements directly on the point. Repeat the firm pressure and circles twice.

Now switch to the left foot. Begin with the transverse colon reflex point, located in the center of the arch. It is not a singular point, so place your thumb over the area and press firmly for three seconds. Release the pressure and switch to a pumping movement for the count of three.

Slide over to the meridian point for the small intestine meridian area, which is beside the descending colon, but slightly to the left. Check the diagram for its exact location. Place your thumb over the area and pump it for five to six seconds. Still using your thumb pad, make small clockwise circles over the entire section. Move your thumb downward to the meridian for the anus, located at the center of the base of the heel. Apply firm pressure to the count of three. Release the pressure and make small clockwise movements directly on the point. Repeat the firm pressure and circles twice.

CHAPTER 7

Aromatherapy Massage

Aromatherapy massage has been around for centuries in other parts of the world. Historians have documented that the Romans and Greeks used aromatherapy massage as part of their royal rituals. In the United States, it has become the current trend. Aromatherapy massage may not have a long history of use in America, but it is here to stay. It is worth mentioning that aromatherapy massage is fast becoming the chosen style for in-home sessions. Thousands of couples across the country are incorporating aromatherapy oils into their private backrubs. It is the chosen way to get a massage.

FUNCTIONS OF AROMATHERAPY MASSAGE

Although aromatherapy massage can be done as a spot treatment, it is most appreciated when it is done for the whole body. Aromatherapy massage simply takes all the stresses and strains out of the body. It works from the outside to the inside of the brain.

NOTE! *In dealing with all skin tissue, the chance for an allergic reaction is very much a concern. Also remember that the recipient's air passages are connected to his or her eyes, ears, and throat. Breathing the essences of a known allergen can bring about serious and severe reactions.*

CHARACTERISTICS OF AROMATHERAPY MASSAGE

There are some similarities between an aromatherapy massage and a standard Swedish massage. Both follow all the typical movements that deal with the muscles of the body. Both can use ointments and/or slippage materials. Aromatherapy is closely linked to holistic health practices.

CHOOSING ESSENTIAL OILS FOR MASSAGE

Essential oils are known to have properties that can affect all the organs inside our bodies.

At least four ounces of oil is needed for a full body aromatherapy massage. The basic formula consists of four ounces of one of the base oils and an additional 10 to 15 drops of the essential oil(s). Base oils "carry" the essential oils into the body. They are the vehicle used to massage the essential oils into the specific body part. Base oils include almond oil, evening primrose oil, peanut oil, sunflower oil, and olive oil. Essential oils include benzoin, carrot, chamomile, jasmine, lavender, lemon, peppermint, and rose. The solution is best received by the skin if it is gently warmed. A baby bottle warmer works best. Keep the beaker inside the warmer for the duration of the massage. This will keep it at a constant warm temperature. You can also run the sides of the beaker under very warm/hot water or put it in a microwave oven for less than five seconds. These last two methods will not keep the oil warm for the duration of the massage.

AROMATHERAPY BODY MASSAGE OIL FORMULAS

With each of these formulas, you begin with a baby bottle warmer and a 120 mL sterile glass beaker. Fill the beaker with 1–1 1/2 inches of water, and bring it to a boil or soft simmer. Place a plastic container in the hot water in which to heat the oils. Do not use the glass beaker to hold the oils. Once you begin the massage, your hands will be oily and grabbing a glass beaker is an accident waiting to happen. The heated water keeps the plastic container warm but not melted. The oil stays warm, but not too hot, and you can lift the plastic container in and out as needed without the fear of shattering glass.

Keeping the oil formulas warm, but not boiling, throughout the session provides a more enjoyable experience for the recipient, and it keeps your hands from getting overly tired. The warmth of the oil helps keep the joints in the fingers more agile.

CAUTION! *Special care must be practiced when using specific oils. Rosemary, sage, eucalyptus, hyssop, fennel, and tagetes (among others) are **very dangerous** to pregnant women. Eucalyptus and lemongrass **cannot be** used on young children. Bergamot is **very dangerous** to anyone with photosensitivity.*

For Dry Skin

Formula 1: Warm 4 oz. apricot kernel oil, add 15 drops geranium, and stir. It is ready to use. This formula will leave the skin smooth with a light, lingering fragrance.

Formula 2: Warm 4 oz. hazelnut oil; add 5 drops jasmine, 5 drops neroli, and 5 drops carrot; and stir. This formula will leave the skin satiny.

Formula 3: Warm 4 oz. jojoba oil, add 7 drops chamomile and 8 drops patchouli; and stir. For sensitive-skinned people, this formula will solve the dryness problem without leaving residue for the skin to feel.

Formula 4: Warm 4 oz. sesame oil, add 15 drops sandalwood, and stir. This formula knows no gender, however most men with dry skin will like this formula best. It has a woodsy fragrance.

Key essential oils for dry skin are benzoin, carrot, chamomile, geranium, hyssop (use sparingly), neroli, patchouli, palmarosa, rose, and sandalwood.

For Oily Skin

Formula 1: Begin with 4 oz. soya bean oil, add 15 drops lemon oil, and stir. This formula will leave the skin refreshed. Perfect for oily skin, since it leaves almost no residue.

Formula 2: Begin with 4 oz. borage seed oil; add 10 drops lavender, 3 drops rosemary, and 2 drops thyme; and stir. The thyme will leave the skin tingly, and the lavender will offer a light, oriental scent.

Formula 3: Begin with 4 oz. grapeseed oil; add 7 drops petitgrain and 8 drops violet leaf oil; and stir. This formulation is very light in fragrance, which is perfect for those who prefer not to have a heavy, lingering scent.

Formula 4: Begin with 4 oz. evening primrose oil, and add 15 drops thyme. This formula will tingle. The sensation will be somewhat like cool heat.

Key essential oils for oily skin are bergamot, eucalyptus, juniper, lavender, lemon oil, palmarosa, patchouli, peppermint, petitgrain, rosemary, sandalwood, thyme, and violet leaf oil.

SPECIAL TIPS AND TRICKS FOR THE PERSON WHO IS "ALLERGIC TO EVERYTHING"

Can the person who is allergic to almost everything enjoy an aromatherapy massage? Yes, it is a proven fact that if you can eat it, it can be put on your skin!

Here are just some of the possibilities: Use regular cooking oil for the base. Vegetable, canola, and corn oil are just a few of the many available oils. Then, instead of mixing essential oils with the base, use pure extracts from the spice section of any grocery store. Pure vanilla, pure ginger, pure cinnamon, pure orange, pure lemon, and pure peach extracts are just a few to choose from.

Vanilla is great for calming. Ginger and cinnamon work for invigorating the skin. Orange extract works well for smokers. Peach is excellent for dry skin. The same 15-drop formulation described in formulas 1 through 4 can be used for these selections.

Quick Reference to the Most Commonly Used Essential Oils

BASIL   USE WITH CARE. Although this herb is used in many food recipes, do NOT assume it is gentle as an aromatherapy oil.

Primary use: To unclog congested, sluggish skin. Works as a natural insect repellent.

BENZOIN   Friar Balsam is a common nickname for this essential oil.

Primary use: To regenerate mature, inelastic skin. It helps to moisturize dry skin. Also good for chapped, dry, and cracked hands. As in all base notes, it is warm and sedating to the skin. The recipient should enjoy this essential oil as it is being massaged on them.

BERGAMOT   *CAUTION:* Extra care must be used because the oil makes the skin photosensitive. Bergamot is never to be used directly or full strength upon the skin. It is strongly suggested that persons wear sunscreens on areas where bergamot is to be used.

Primary use: For all oily skin and hair, and for seborrhea of the scalp. Acne conditions and rosacea also respond well to it. If you know that the person is an active outdoors person and will not use sun protection, choose another essential oil for your formula. Anyone who applies this essential oil as part of a treatment, must also protect their own hands with a sunscreen.

CAMPHOR   *CAUTION:* It must not be used during pregnancy. Very small amounts should be used. Where 4–5 drops of other oils would be fine, 1–3 drops will do nicely for this one.

Primary use: For oily skin and hair. If used, is generally included in products that are washed off; such as cleansers, shampoos, and masks rather than moisturizers.

CARROT   This essential oil has the power to stain the skin, nails, and scalp. Care must be taken not to use it "neat" (straight on the skin).

Primary use: For all skin, hair, and nail care that needs revitalizing and moisturizing. It also has a calming effect on the skin and cuticles.

CEDARWOOD   With its natural woodsy aroma, this essential oil will appeal to men and anyone else who enjoys the smell of the outdoors. However, anyone with allergies to wood spurs and other forest elements will not do well with this essential oil.

Primary use: Hair care: this essential oil is helpful in treating alopecia, dandruff, and seborrhea of the scalp. Skin care: for oily skin and irritations.

CHAMOMILE GERMAN   It is particularly mild and gentle and can be used on young children. You will find that this essential oil has broad appeal for its natural aroma and versatile usage.

Primary use: For all skin and nails that are sensitive, dry, or irritated. This essential oil is very effective with cracked or chapped nails. Use on scalps that are dry or flaky. Capillary distention such as couperose, is helped. It will also soothe acne and eczema.

CHAMOMILE ROMAN   Used similarly to chamomile German. It also shares its treatment selection variety and broad appeal.

CINNAMON   A very potent essential oil. Use very sparingly. Too much in skin potions can cause irritations. Not to be used "neat," or unadulterated. It performs well in blends where it is just a small part of the formula.

Primary use: Skin and nail care: It works very well to tone the skin, and as an antiviral in skin and nails.

CLARY SAGE   This herb works very quickly on the body in many different applications. It does not have a strong positive or negative response to its aroma. It is not a scent that is widely recognized upon first contact.

Primary use: On mature skin to perk up the complexion, as a cell regenerator. It soothes any skin or nails that are inflamed. Stimulates hair growth and helps to regulate seborrhea of the scalp.

CLOVE   A very powerful and potent essential oil, so use only the tiniest of drops. Most people are aware of it as a spice in cooking, and many will have a predetermined idea as to whether they like its natural aroma. Ask before selecting this as part of a blended formula.

Primary use: Helps fight bacteria in nails and skin.

CYPRESS Another woodsy aroma that will have a certain appeal to outdoor lovers, but check on the possibility of allergies to tree pollens, before selecting this oil.

Primary use: Toning the body, balancing oily skin, strengthening nails. Works as an antiseptic to all skin and nails, oxygenates broken capillaries.

EUCALYPTUS, EUCALYPTUS LEMON, EUCALYPTUS PEPPER-MINT, EUCALYPTUS RADIATA *CAUTION:* Do not use on young children, or anyone with even the mildest asthmatic condition. This oil's aroma does not blend in with other essential oils' aromas. It will always dominate the blend's smell. One drop of this essential oil can equal the aroma power of 10 drops of other less aromatic selections. Once again, ask about the person's preference to its smell. Many will relate its aroma to medicinal products used in their youths.

Primary use: Acne and oily skin. Great for increasing the circulation of the nail beds and cuticles. Superb scalp stimulator. An excellent antiseptic.

EVERLASTING Similar to eucalyptus, this oil's aroma does not blend in with the aromas of other essential oils. It will always dominate the blend's smell. Once again, ask about the person's preference to its smell.

Primary use: It has strong anti-inflammatory properties that are wonderful on sensitive skin; acne conditions; or any inflamed nails, cuticles, or skin.

FENNEL (sweet) *CAUTION:* Use with care and never during pregnancy. Inside the herb is a high phenolic ether content, thus a very small amount is to be used in the formula. It is hard to predict a person's response to the aroma. It can go either way. Most often, the formula will only have one drop of this essential oil.

Primary use: For cleansers for oily skin. To revitalize mature skin and hands.

FRANKINCENSE Not as pungent as eucalyptus, but it will still dominate the blend's aroma. Check the recipient's preference. It will not be as recognizable as eucalyptus. Only those who are more experienced in aromatherapy will find themselves turning to this essential oil a lot.

Primary use: Skincare: For calming any inflamed tissue and for toning loose skin. Nails: Excellent for treating damaged cuticles. Hair: Adds body to limp hair.

GERANIUM Its natural aroma has broad appeal for women of all ages. Most often men will find the aroma of this essential oil too flowery.

Primary use: Multifunctional. Can be effective as a cell generator for mature skin or an astringent for oily skin, and can decrease the slick found on acne skin. Offers quick repair for chapped, cracked hands and cuticles. Helps reduce the greasy hair sensation.

GRAPEFRUIT It has large universal appeal, partly due to its over-whelmingly popular aroma, and for its wide-ranging abilities.

Primary use: Uniformly used for hair, skin, and nails. No one area is stronger than the others. Hair: It reduces the slick formed by seborrhea, and reduces dandruff scales. It increases the fresh bounce to most hair. Skin: It works to tone facial and body tissue, especially tissue with cellulite. Nails: It brightens yellow nails, helps increase the oxygen flow to nails to rid buildup of residue on the nail beds. It strengthens the cuticle tissue.

HYSSOP *CAUTION:* Must be used with care, because it is such a strong oil. It cannot be used during pregnancy. This herb's natural aroma may not be on everyone's top ten list. Check with the recipient first. Very small amounts of oil are used in any formula. For most formulas, the maximum number of drops will be two.

Primary use: For moisturizing any sensitive skin and reducing redness of couperose. Excellent for treating eczema of the scalp and skin. Will treat hands and feet for weak nails or damaged cuticles.

JASMINE A solvent, often ether, must be used to extract the oil out of the flower, which increases the cost of the essential oil. Careful selection of the pure absolute of the jasmine flower will assure the proper oil for use. Only very small amounts of the oil are required. This flower has a strong oriental aroma, and the reaction to it will be close to 50–50, positive or negative. Those who suffer greatly from hayfever-style allergies might not have a positive reaction to this oil.

Primary use: It has exceptional versatility. In some formulations it will reduce the oily slick off of skin and hair. In other formulations it can be an overall moisturizer for dry skin, scalp, and nails. Due to its gentle nature, it works well with all sensitive bodies, hands, and feet.

JUNIPER In ancient times it was the antiseptic of choice. It was considered the rubbing alcohol of the aromatherapy world.

Primary use: Still used as an active antiseptic for all skin and body areas, including the hands and feet. It is often part of the toning formulations for treating cellulite and flabby arms. In skin care, many acne conditions are improved and oily skin reduces its sebum levels.

LAVENDER   Its aroma makes this essential oil very popular with all ages. It has a fine calming reaction to the internal and external parts of the body.

Primary use: This essential oil can be used on all parts of the body, even the eyes and lips. Hair: To treat alopecia and dry, brittle hair. Skin: Acne, rosacea, and oily skins respond well to lavender. Most inflammation of the skin, as well as psoriasis, is reduced. On mature skin, it aids in moisture. For the hands and feet, it works beautifully to soothe and relieve chapping and cracking.

LEMON   *CAUTION:* Keep away from area directly around the eyes. It tops the list as the most favored essential oil, due to the powerful aroma of the fruit and its wide appeal with men and women alike. It would be very hard to find a person who does not like the natural fragrance of this oil.

Primary use: One of the most flexible oils of all. It can be used on every body part from the top of the scalp and hair, to the bottoms of the feet. Depending on how it is mixed, it works with oily or dry skin. It energizes the mature skin and repairs wrinkled skin to a new smoothness. For nails it clears yellowing and refreshes the nail beds and cuticles.

LEMONGRASS   *CAUTIONS:* Do not use this on children. Do not use directly on the skin. Do not use on clients who are allergic to grass pollens. This essential oil is also known for its antiseptic properties. However, it can act as an irritant if it is applied directly on the skin and should not be used straight, or "neat." In blends, use just a little of this essential oil. For most formulas, do not go over the four-drop level.

Primary use: Predominantly used in body care, for toning, and as an antiseptic. Also used on acne or oily skin to reduce pustules—but only as a blend, not straight.

LIME   *CAUTION:* Keep away from the eyes. A close choice to its cousin the lemon, its natural aroma is strongly popular with men. It is not as diversified as the lemon and is not used as often.

Primary use: On the skin as an astringent and tonic.

MARJORAM   Although it is colorless, it is also very pungent. It does not appeal to everyone. Ask before selecting this essential oil for your blend.

Primary use: For treating bruising of any tissue or black-and-blue marks on the scalp, skin, hands, and feet. For damaged nail beds, such as "blackened nails," it has a positive healing quality.

MELISSA   Clients will either find this essential oil very pleasant smelling or be repelled by its aroma. Check first before making your blend.

Primary use: Nails and feet: It is a wonderful antifungal solution. Skin: Depending on the blend of the formula, acne and eczema are aided, and mature skin can be regenerated. This essential oil can be custom fit into oily or dry skin treatments.

MYRRH   A hormonal oil, this essential oil is highly recognized for its involvement in biblical history. Due to its connection, this oil has a strong aura surrounding it. People may respond from a deep emotional reaction to this oil, based solely on its connection to Jesus.

Primary use: Skin: Regenerates and revitalizes mature skin. For any skin that is red and sore looking, it acts as an anti-inflammatory. Nails: Reduces redness in dry, cracked hands and cuticles. Hair: Acts as an anti-inflammatory oil for scalps.

NEROLI   It has a pale yellow color. Its aroma is particularly strong and will be pleasant to many people.

Primary use: Hair: Treats scalps that are sore, or cracked and picked at. Nails: Treats bitten and torn cuticles or reddened, cracked hands and feet. Skin: Treats skin that is showing signs of irritation. This oil is perfect for treating sensitive skin.

NIAOULI   Its natural aura is very similar to lavender, which makes it very popular with most people.

Primary use: As a broad-spectrum antiseptic solution. Skin: Improves acne and oily skin. Feet: Treats any cuts and sores.

ORANGE   It is very mild, which makes it a good choice for children and anyone with sensitive skin. Its aroma makes it one of the most popular essential oils.

Primary use: Hair: It makes the hair silky smooth and shiny. Nails: It is perfect for treating rough, dry hands and feet. If the skin is weak and flabby-looking, it will revitalize it. Skin: Reduces oil and acne conditions. It helps treat congested skin. On mature skin, it improves tone and smoothness.

OREGANO   This is a strong essential oil. It has to be used very sparingly. The aroma is so connected to food, that people may actually get hungry when the blend is created. It has broad appeal for both men and women.

Primary use: Body: It works very well on cellulite. Nails: It brightens the nail beds.

PALMAROSA   This essential oil is extremely versatile. The only possible limitation will be for those with allergies to pollens and grasses. The aroma is neither engaging nor repelling.

Primary use: Hair: It is effective in reducing limp hair. Nails: Revitalizes dry, cracked hands and nails. Also good for tired feet that are dry and flaky. Skin: It energizes mature, wrinkled skin.

PARSLEY   This essential oil's appeal is based on its overall acceptance in food preparation. It helps the body clear itself of toxins.

Primary use: An effective antiseptic for skin, nails, and feet. Skin: It is effective on couperose and it tones skin. Hair: It helps rid cigarette toxins from the follicles.

PATCHOULI   This oil has the ability to perform two different actions based on the quantity of the oil. Very few drops will energize, whereas many drops will relax. The exact reason is not known.

Primary use: As part of its ability to work in different reactions, it is excellent for cracked, dry hands and feet. Skin: Oily and acne skin conditions are improved and put back into balance. Hair: Restores body to oily hair.

PEPPERMINT   A very powerful essential oil, partly due to its cellular composition and partly due to its aroma. A strong favorite with young people. It can overwhelm the formula if its percentage of drops is significantly higher than the others. However, it can also create a popular aroma when mixed with other essential oils that have aromas that are not as pleasant.

Primary use: A major aid in reducing inflammation, irritation, and couperose. Ashy coloring of skin from smoking or prolonged sickness will brighten. On oily or acne skin, it helps reduce the congestion. Hair: It is a major tool in stimulating the scalp and loosening scales of dandruff and eczema. Nails: With its ability to oxygenate the area, it helps nails restore a healthy coloring.

PETITGRAIN   It is not as favorable in aroma as its sister oil, neroli.

Primary use: It works as a great balancer for oily conditions. Skin: Reduces oily sebum slicks and waxy buildup on acne skin. Hair: Reduces the greasy sensation on hair and scalp.

ROSE BULGAR and **ROSE MAROC**   The potent aroma of rose oil makes it one of the most powerful and most loved by women. It is not favored by most men. It is so gentle that it can be used on the most sensitive skins and on very young children.

Primary use: For treating all sensitive skin that is dry. On mature skin it helps reduce the signs of aging. On oily skin it reduces redness. It has a calming effect on any couperose. It soothes rough, cracked, and dry conditions on hands and feet.

ROSEMARY   *CAUTION:* Because it naturally possesses ketones of camphor, never use it under any conditions on a pregnant woman. The best rosemary oil will be costly and worth it! It is a natural cleanser of toxins, reducer of sebum, and a cellular regenerator. This makes this essential oil one of the most diverse.

Primary use: Hair: Alopecia, dandruff, and seborrhea of the scalp all improve with use. Skin: Oily plugs and acne conditions lessen. On mature skin the cells perk up, become less wrinkled. Nails: Feet and hands will gain smoothness and increase in circulation with use.

SAGE   *CAUTION:* It should not be used on pregnant women. Be careful when using sage in a blend. Its aroma may not mix well with everything.

Primary use: Hair: It is effective in reducing alopecia. Skin: It works to unclog congested skin, or improve skin that has a tendency to be sluggish.

SANDALWOOD   The woodsy aroma makes it particularly popular with men and many active, outdoor-loving women. It would be wise to check if the person has a history of allergies to grasses, trees, and pollens, before choosing this oil.

Primary use: It works as a terrific antiseptic and antifungal solution. Nails: This is great for any nail care needs when dealing with fungus. Skin: Perfect for treating dry, cracked hands or feet. It also works on dry, mature, wrinkled conditions. Hair: It is added to solutions to increase moisture in brittle hair.

SPEARMINT   Its minty aroma makes it a hit with most people. It has an uplifting effect.

Primary use: It is used as a body toning oil.

TAGETES   *CAUTION:* This essential oil must be used with extreme care. It is toxic if used directly on the skin, hands, and feet. Never use during pregnancy, as it has a naturally abortive reaction.

Primary use: With all the warnings of its being toxic, if used in a very diluted blend, it is extremely effective when treating athlete's foot and any fungal infections of the nails.

TEA TREE   This essential oil has a very pungent aroma and, by itself, is not particularly appealing. It has strong antiseptic and antifungal properties and works well in all areas of the body.

Primary use: Hair: On the scalp it is very effective in controlling dandruff and any irritations. Skin: Improves acne conditions and reduces excess sebum. It is one of nature's best ointments for herpes. Nails: It works incredibly well to control nail fungus.

THYME (Sweet and Lemon)   Both oils work very well as antibiotics, antiseptics, and antifungals.

Primary use: Due to their special properties, they are extremely effective during a pedicure. Treats any fungal infections on the nails, hands, and feet. Used as an antiseptic for the scalp and skin.

VIOLET LEAF   It has a very light and pleasant aroma, which makes it particularly favorable with mature women. It is a relatively mild oil.

Primary use: Skin and nails: It is used to moisturize skin on the body, face, hands, and feet. It softens the appearance of wrinkles on mature skin.

YLANG-YLANG The grades of oil available for aromatherapy are of a lesser quality. They tend to resemble jasmine in fragrance, although they are not quite as distinct. Its aroma can be repelling to some; therefore, check before adding it to the blend. As in all tree oils, check for allergies to tree pollens before deciding to use this essential oil.

Primary use: Hair: It helps to degrease oily hair and scalp. Skin: Can help control acne and oily skin conditions. Nails: During pedicures, ylang-ylang acts to soften rough calluses.

Index

Note: The letter "f" following a page number indicates a figure.